HIGHLINE COMMUNITY COLLEGE LIBRARY
3 0090 00005328 U
944.07092 N216w
The mortal Napoleon III

D0407575

The Mortal Napoleon III

THE MORTAL
Napoleon III

Roger L. Williams

PRINCETON UNIVERSITY PRESS
PRINCETON, NEW JERSEY

L. C. Card: 75-155005
ISBN: 0-691-05192-5

This book has been composed in Granjon with Garamond display
Printed in the United States of America
by Princeton University Press, Princeton, New Jersey

Contents

Illustrations

Frontispiece: From a portrait of the aging Napoleon III by an unknown photographer. I bought a copy of this photograph fifteen years ago as a curiosity in Biarritz, later discovering that the same pose had served as the model for a painting in the possession of Dr. Mercier des Rochettes entitled *Napoleon III on the Terrace of the Villa Eugénie*. This villa was the imperial residence at Biarritz.

Facing page 12: Portrait of Napoleon III in the uniform of a division general, by Flandrin, in the Versailles Museum, reproduced by permission of Giraudon.

The Mortal Napoleon III

I should rather know the truth of the talk he had in his tent with one of his close friends on the eve of the battle than the speech he made the next day to his army, and what he did in his study or in his own room than what he did in public and in the Senate.

Montaigne

Introduction

This book is a biographical study, not a biography. Napoleon III himself is one of the major remaining mysteries in the history of the Second Empire, and his health in particular, never clearly understood, has traditionally been held to have been responsible for the defects of his governance. That he was ill from the earliest years of his reign was generally known both at home and abroad, just as it has always been known that he was physically unfit for the campaign against Prussia in 1870 and that he died in 1873 after a series of operations to crush an unusually large bladder stone. The emperor's well-known secretiveness helped to obscure his true state from those around him and contributed to widespread speculation about the nature of his maladies and their effect upon his ability to govern.

Octave Aubry, whose studies of the Second Empire are still standard fare in France, gives us a typical picture of the unfortunate emperor: inactive and slow-moving as he aged; suffering from gout and renal troubles which left him depressed; treated with opiates that increased his sluggishness; too fond of women, who wore him down; with snow-white hair continually dyed to create the illusion of energy and good health.[1] Physicians, too, have described the case of this most famous patient in the history of urology, taking a professional interest in the influence of disease upon history. "In later life," Dr. S. F. Marwood writes, he "did display weakness and irresolution, . . . and I believe that these defects, which he masked behind an inscrutable demeanour, were due in no small part to the chronic debilitating and often incapacitating illness which dogged him through the greater part of his reign, and which indeed became almost unbearable in his closing years." As for 1870, Dr. Marwood added that "this sick man, mind clouded and judgment impaired by pain and toxaemia, decided on war and gave the order to mobilise."[2] These two views, one from an historian and one from a physician, are merely cited as representative

[1] Octave Aubry, *The Second Empire,* New York: D. Appleton, 1940, pp. 306-307.

[2] Dr. S. F. Marwood, "Louis Napoleon and his Doctors," *Medical Journal of the Southwest* (Bristol), LXXXII (January, 1967), 71-72, 76.

of the literature on Napoleon's condition, since the primary justification for the present volume is the inadequacy of such traditional portraits.

Though Napoleon III's medical record is presented in the subsequent chapters as chronologically as possible, to enable readers to sense what his contemporaries really knew of his condition—and how the record was amplified in the decades after his death—it does no harm to alert readers in advance that the case was more complicated than is generally known. Arthritis, hemorrhoids, gout, prostatitis, and several renal disorders appear at various stages in his life; and we have to consider also the possibility that he suffered from diabetes.

My intention, however, has not been to limit the study to those facts we might generally call medical, but to look at Napoleon the man. As Erik H. Erikson has pointed out, Freud's most important contribution to modern medicine lay not in those formulas about personality development that we call Freudian, but in a "technique of observation." If we are really to understand or to appreciate the men who have affected history, we must endeavor to observe them as complete individuals. To that task we have to bring, beyond the historian's ability to evaluate sources, the resolve to be open-minded and objective. As our ability to see others depends in no small way upon both our readiness and ability to see ourselves honestly, this particular genre of history seems fraught with special peril.[3] That we can never know the absolute truth about another individual, living or dead, constitutes

[3] Lucian W. Pye, "Personal Identity and Political Ideology," *Psychoanalysis and History*, ed. by Bruce Mazlish, Englewood Cliffs, New Jersey: Prentice-Hall, 1963, p. 170.

a lesser hazard in embarking upon such research, because we are forced to recognize at the outset that we are engaged in an essay in probability.

We historians have not been alone in our traditional reluctance to accept medical evidence. Physicians, too, know how easy it can be to exaggerate the influence of disease upon an individual; one of them, who has otherwise been generously helpful to me in my study, has written that "medical men [should] be ready to protest at being jockeyed into a false position by superficial historians." It is only fair to record, therefore, that this particular physician thought that Napoleon III's case was interesting, but that it did not involve "any startling or dramatic features and certainly . . . no disclosures of a psychiatric character so attractive nowadays to the lay writer."[4] The validity of my dissent will, of course, be judged by each reader, as I propose to show that the most significant of the emperor's ailments was a neurosis that he overcame. But the neurosis reveals to us the origin of a major problem that in fact did affect the history of the Second Empire.

Even on a more general level, historians have been somewhat neglectful of the influence of disease upon the history of mankind. Although we readily accept as factual the devastating impact of a plague upon a society, we have been slower to recognize that, since many of the diseases from which we suffer as individuals are unknown in the state of nature, history and disease are in fact inseparable. To a significant degree this unhappy equation

[4] Dr. Macdonald Critchley, "A Medical History of Napoleon III," *Second Empire Medley*, ed. by W. H. Holden, London: British Technical and General Press, 1952, p. 24.

came about because evolution did not prepare our diencephalon (that part of the brain-stem that regulates bodily activity) for that artificial environment we call civilization. Some of these diseases, gout for example, merit the historian's special interest because of a notable predilection for people of power and wealth, so that they are in the forefront of those diseases that have influenced the history of civilization.[5]

As the reader will soon discover, this volume is arranged topically, the chapters having distinct characters as the topics vary, but also because the sources available for the topics vary greatly in number and character. The first three chapters amount to an introduction to the final three, preparing the reader for the intricate details of the emperor's diseases and politics. The first chapter, a mosaic, delves into his personality, mind, and character, his attitude toward medicine, and the motives behind his marital choice. The second chapter investigates his rather notorious love-life as a further key to his character and his medical state, and the third chapter surveys the imperial medical service.

The bibliography does not include all the sources cited in the footnotes, but is specially designed for students of the Second Empire. In addition to the sources listed, I have received help, advice, and information from a number of people and institutions. I want to acknowledge that assistance with the warmest thanks here, while taking the customary pledge of responsibility myself for the interpretations in the book. This is no mere formality, as the

[5] Dr. W. S. C. Copeman, *A Short History of the Gout and the Rheumatic Diseases*, Berkeley and Los Angeles: University of California Press, 1964, p. vii.

very nature of the book means that it could not have been written without consultation, and because I know that not all the consultants will agree with everything that follows. My thanks to the staff of the Archives Nationales in Paris; to the staff of the Bibliothèque Nationale in Paris, and notably to the Manuscript Division; to Mme. Harburger and M. Coutarel of the Archives de la Préfecture de Police in Paris; to le Médecin Général Inspecteur Favre, le Médecin Général Inspecteur Pareire, M. Vialard, and Mme. Laprun of the Archives du Val-de-Grâce in Paris; to Mr. L. M. Payne, Librarian of the Royal College of Physicians in London; to Dr. Macdonal Critchley of the Institute of Neurology in London; to Dr. S. F. Marwood of Bristol; to Dr. William Slocum Davenport, Jr., of Paris; to Professor T.A.B. Corley of the University of Reading in Berkshire; to Mme. Olivier Ziegel of Paris, who efficiently tracked down medical sources before my arrival; to Dr. Preston K. Munter of Harvard University; to Dr. Robert L. Becker of Santa Barbara, California; to Dr. Robert J. Kurth of Houston, Texas; to Colonel Jack R. Robison, M.D., and Dr. Ray Fitch, Lackland Air Force Base, Texas; and finally to several colleagues at the University of California, Santa Barbara: Professors Barbara B. DeWolfe, Bruce Rickborn, and Leonard M. Marsak.

Roger L. Williams
Santa Barbara, California

He was vastly superior to what his preceding career and his mad enterprises might very properly have led one to believe of him.

Alexis de Tocqueville

1 *The Imperial Patient*

Prince Louis-Napoleon was the third son of King Louis and Queen Hortense of Holland, the last child of an unfortunate dynastic marriage that had been forced in 1802 by Napoleon Bonaparte, then First Consul, six years after his own marriage to Josephine Beauharnais. Louis, then twenty-four, was Napoleon's younger and favorite brother; Hortense, nineteen, was Josephine's daughter by a first marriage. Whatever political cynicism may have induced the First Consul to insist upon the marriage, and whatever pleasure Josephine may have taken in seeing her own position ratified by the new alliance, both of them knew that Louis and Hortense had no taste for each other. On the other hand, Louis had virtually been reared by Napoleon, who had high hopes for him, and the lovely Hortense showed promise in music and sketching. It could be hoped that they would learn to appreciate each others' qualities after marriage. But it was not to be, and the wonder is that they produced three children.

The marital failure was chiefly Louis's fault. As an adolescent he had been alert and affectionate, full of admiration for his brother Napoleon. But as he approached twenty, which is to say shortly after Napoleon's marriage to Josephine, he began to exhibit those qualities which would make him infamous as a husband and father: moodiness, moroseness, secretiveness, irresolution, with a pronounced solicitude for his health. Indeed, he became a serious hypochondriac. Today there is reason to think that the root of the problem was Louis's suppressed homosexual attraction to Napoleon, something that Josephine suspected at the time. Louis's attempts to be manly led to an attack of venereal disease in his twentieth year, leaving him permanently afflicted by what was probably gonorrheal arthritis and enhancing the hypochondria. Faced with marriage to Hortense, he sulked at length before going through the ceremony on March 3, 1802.

Napoleon then began to groom Louis for administrative duty and high rank. In 1804 he was named a general and to the Council of State. The following year he was made Governor of Paris and in 1806 he became king of Holland. Meanwhile, his delusions of persecution increased and he gave way to fits of jealousy, accusing his wife of sexual relations first with Napoleon and later with other men.[1] Moreover, his governance in Holland seemed calculated to infuriate Napoleon, opening a period of bad relations between the two brothers. Hortense did seek comfort and affection elsewhere, though not with Napoleon, but her three sons credited to King Louis were without doubt legitimate whatever the rumors to the contrary. Napoleon-Charles, born late in 1802, died of croup in 1807. The second son, Napoleon-Louis, was born in 1804; Charles-Louis-Napoleon, later Napoleon III, was born April 20, 1808. As is well known, Hortense also bore an illegitimate child in 1811, who was given the name Morny.

Napoleon's announcement in 1809 that he would divorce Josephine encouraged Louis to ask permission to divorce Hortense, which was denied. The upshot was that Louis abandoned his Dutch throne in 1810 and fled to Bohemia, beginning a permanent separation from Hortense. After 1815 he moved to Italy, living chiefly in Florence and Rome until his death in 1846. He never recovered the health and charm of his youth, and his niece recorded the sordid details of the proposal of matrimony he made as an old man to a very young girl that is clearly a matter for psychopathology.[2]

After having been abandoned in 1810, Queen Hortense requested and received permission to return to Paris with her two sons. Having already lost one child, she was the more concerned for her last-born, who had been so feeble

[1] Ernest Jones, "The Case of Louis Bonaparte," *Journal of Abnormal Psychology*, VIII (December 1913-January 1914), 291-300.

[2] Princess Mathilde Bonaparte, "Souvenirs des années d'exil," *Revue des deux mondes*, XLII (Dec. 15, 1927), 742-744.

at birth that he was bathed in wine and wrapped in cotton to bring him to life. Evidently she sensed that she, too, might be dying; and even though they both survived, she afterwards had extraordinary fears and premonitions about his safety and health.[3] He could hardly avoid being a pampered child. A year after his birth, another child was born in the household, Albine-Hortense Lacroix. The parents were in Queen Hortense's service, and the infant Louis-Napoleon was named godfather for the newborn baby. In time she became his playmate, loving him like a brother.[4]

Evidently Queen Hortense had hoped that her third child would be a girl, and for some time after his birth Louis-Napoleon was dressed and treated as a girl. His playmate would later remember him as an attractive child, more like a girl than a boy. He early learned to dissimulate, especially to hide his feelings.[5] We do not know precisely when Queen Hortense permitted the child to become a boy, but there has never been any doubt that she was absorbed in him during those years of personal and political disquiet. Their closeness became even more pronounced after Waterloo when Hortense not only had to leave France, but was obliged to surrender Napoleon-Louis, her elder child, to King Louis after he initiated a scandalous suit against her. With Louis-Napoleon she wandered in exile for many months

[3] *Mémoires de la Reine Hortense*, Paris: Plon, 1927, II, 3-4.

[4] Marcel Emerit, *Madame Cornu et Napoléon III*, Paris: Les Presses Modernes, 1937, pp. 4-10.

[5] Mme. Cornu to N. W. Senior, "Louis-Napoleon Painted by a Contemporary," *Cornhill Magazine*, XXVII (Jan.-June, 1873), 603; and Emerit, *op. cit.*, pp. 146-147.

before settling permanently in 1817 in Switzerland, having bought Arenenberg Castle in the canton of Türgau, near the Lake of Constance.

To have lost a father like King Louis might seem to have been supportable; but for the rest of his life, Louis-Napoleon's extraordinary devotion to his mother affected his attitude to women, which perhaps the presence of a decent father could have altered. It is true, of course, that Hortense, a favorite of Napoleon I, endeavored to imbue her child with a sense of his Napoleonic destiny as a father might have done. But boys whose mothers are absorbed in them, if they do not develop a physical indifference or hostility to women, are apt to become promiscuous, as was to be the case of Louis-Napoleon. Even promiscuity implies a certain contempt for women, except for the mother or the wife who is thought to be different from the rest of them.

Hortense often crossed into Italy to spend the coldest months of the winter, and on such a visit in 1823 she permitted Louis-Napoleon to visit his father in Florence. King Louis's conception of his paternal obligations may be measured by the rules he set down for his fifteen-year-old son:

1) Holidays are strictly limited to Thursdays and Sundays. On Thursdays he must write to his mother, and he may not leave his room until the letter is written, *well written.*

2) He may drink only Bordeaux—no coffee or liquors.

3) He will wash his feet once a week, his nails with lemon, his hands with bran, but must never use soap.

4) He is forbidden the use of colognes and all other scents.

5) When at the theater, he will always put on his cape before leaving his box.

6) His shoes will always be made large.

7) He must keep his head clean with a dry sponge—no water.

8) His suspenders must always be very long so that he can hold himself upright.

9) He must care for his own wardrobe and his money.

10) He must obey even an unjust order.

11) Chocolate will be kept in a locked place. One quarter of a bar is the most he may have each day.[6]

This for a young man who was already quite mature and who was rumored to have seduced a village girl in Switzerland the year before. We get a later picture of him in Rome at the age of twenty-one, a portrait of Hortense's influence: "a wild harum-scarum youth" galloping heedlessly about the streets, fencing and pistol-shooting, without any apparent serious thought except for the conviction that he would someday rule France. He was very athletic and muscular, with an oddly grave face but an unusually bright and captivating smile.[7]

On the surface nothing suggested the fulfillment of a Napoleonic destiny. Yet, with him, appearances always deceived. At the age of twenty-four he published his first political pamphlet, *Rêveries politiques* (1832); he continued this self-advertisement with *Considérations politiques et militaires sur la Suisse* (1833). When the author-

[6] Dr. Augustin Cabanès, *Moeurs intimes du passé* (8th series), *Education de princes*, Paris: A. Michel, 1923, pp. 518-519.

[7] James Howard Harris, third Earl of Malmesbury, *Memoirs of an Ex-Minister*, London: Longmans, Green, 1884-1885, I, 33.

ities in the canton of Türgau responded by making him a captain in the Swiss militia, Louis-Napoleon drew up a *Manuel d'Artillerie* (1835) as a guide for Swiss officers, which also served as a prelude to his attempt to seize power in France, an attempt that ended in fiasco at Strasbourg on October 30, 1836. His second attempt to gain the French throne took place on August 6, 1840, when he landed at Boulogne. Easily captured, he was not simply deported as before but was brought before the Chamber of Peers, which sentenced him to life imprisonment in the fortress of Ham. He was registered at the fortress as being thirty-two years old, five feet six inches in height, with a slight curvature of the spine (one of King Louis's notable features).[8] Several of his companions were also sentenced to terms at Ham: General Charles Montholon, an intellectual lightweight who had shared Napoleon I's captivity on Saint Helena; and Dr. Henri Conneau, who had formerly been in the service of Queen Hortense, but who had joined Louis-Napoleon after her death in 1837. A valet, Charles Thélin, was authorized to reside there, and before long the government agreed that the Prince might enjoy the consolation of occasional female companions.[9]

The period at Ham (he would escape in 1846) worked remarkable changes on his mind and body. He had published another important pamphlet before his captivity, *Des Idées napoléoniennes* in 1839; now at Ham he conscientiously tried to keep his intellect alive through constant study. Hortense Lacroix, now Madame Cornu,

[8] T.A.B. Corley, *Democratic Despot; a Life of Napoleon III*, London: Barrie and Rockliff, 1961, pp. 2-4.

[9] *Ibid.*, pp. 43-46; and Emerit, *op. cit.*, pp. 14-19.

brought her husband on seven different trips between 1841 and 1845 to visit her childhood friend, and by 1843 she was convinced that he was becoming a new man. No longer simply a fine gentleman with a destiny, but a man with new intellectual vigor and breadth thanks to wide reading, scientific experimenting, and writing. From this period came his *Fragments historiques*, his *Extinction du paupérisme*, and his study on the construction of a canal across Nicaragua.[10] Among his visitors was Louis Blanc in 1844, who came at the invitation of Louis-Napoleon to discuss social and political ideas. Instead of the harum-scarum youth, Blanc found a pensive prisoner, walking with slow steps in the limited area assigned for his exercise, head inclined, speaking in a low voice so as not to be overheard by the guard who followed close behind. Blanc also remembered trying to convince Louis-Napoleon that only a republic would be possible in the future, something he would stress again in an open letter to President Bonaparte dated August 10, 1849, republished shortly after the coup d'état of 1851.[11]

As for Louis-Napoleon's health, it is clear that the confinement at Ham did him no good. In 1858, Louis Blanc would recall that Louis-Napoleon had been comfortably housed at Ham,[12] but no contemporary reports suggests that the fortress was anything other than damp and miserable. The rheumatism he presumably acquired there lasted the rest of his life. Probably the lack of exercise

[10] Malmesbury, *op. cit.*, 1, 158-159.

[11] Louis Blanc, *L'Empire moins l'empereur, lettre à Louis Bonaparte*, n.p., ca. 1851, pp. 5-6.

[12] In his *1848, Historical Revelations*, London: Chapman & Hall, 1858.

was even more serious for a man who had been athletic. On July 11, 1843, he described his physical misery in a letter to Madame Cornu: "For four or five months, I have had headaches nearly every day; it comes from the sedentary life I lead. I am going to subject myself to a strict diet, for this headache may have its cause in my stomach. It makes me sluggish."[13] Lord Malmesbury found him dreadfully weary of prison during his half-day visit on April 20, 1845, and fearful that opportunities to escape were deliberately provided by the government in order to create an occasion to shoot him.[14] Thirteen months later, however, with the aid of Dr. Conneau he contrived an escape, using as his justification the refusal of the July Monarchy to allow him to visit his dying father. King Louis did die two months later in Florence, before Louis-Napoleon reached him from London.

After this graduation from what Louis-Napoleon later called the University of Ham, he seemed older than his thirty-eight years. Descriptions by eye witnesses of his figure and his movements make us realize that portraits of him painted in the eighteen-fifties or sixties conveyed a flattering image, for his body was ungainly and ill-proportioned, and his swaying gait ungraceful.[15] His legs were too short for his body, he had begun to walk slowly, feet toed out, his head usually slightly inclined to the left. When he wanted to move faster, his arm and shoulder movements were exaggerated. His hands were large

[13] Blanchard Jerrold, *The Life of Napoleon III*, 4 vols., London: Longmans, Green, 1874-1882, II, 422.

[14] Malmesbury, *op. cit.*, I, 158.

[15] Anna L. Bicknell, *Life in the Tuileries Under the Second Empire*, London: T. Fisher Unwin, 1895, p. 36.

and muscular, but the thumbs were noticeably stubby. When he stood still to talk to you, he usually inclined a bit to the right or to the left rather than directly facing you. The neck was too thick, especially unattractive in a small man but another sign that he was, or had been, a powerful man. It was in his back and neck that he most resembled the Bonapartes, especially when he was on horseback. He rode well and was impressive in the saddle, but he looked his worst during the Second Empire, when he would on occasion wear the white breeches and silk stockings of the First Empire.[16]

Yet he was an attractive man, pleasing to those who knew him, and his face and manner usually awed bystanders. His eyes seemed small, and he often appeared to be preoccupied; but his expression was usually kindly and could change to a gentle and even a maliciously ironical expression in the presence of members of his household. But when meeting people on matters of state he would become instantly grave and serious.[17] This self-control became as celebrated as it was baffling, even to those who saw him regularly year after year. One of his relatives who both liked and admired him as emperor said that he always excited her curiosity, "for who can say that he *knows* the emperor?"[18] She thought of him as a wonderful enigma to be deciphered.

This deceptive exterior he developed as a child and per-

[16] Sir William Augustus Fraser, *Napoleon III (My Recollections)*, London: Sampson, Low, Marston, 1896, pp. 7-10.

[17] Dr. Ernest Barthez de Marmorières, *La Famille impériale à Saint-Cloud et à Biarritz*, Paris: Calmann-Lévy, 1913, pp. 71-72.

[18] Comtesse Stéphanie de Tascher de la Pagerie, *Mon séjour aux Tuileries, 1852-1858*, Paris: Ollendorff, 1893, I, 179.

fected over the years so that, in reading some of his contemporaries, we come to think of him as silent and passionless. He may have had a calm crust but, as Madame Cornu remarked in 1858, "furious Italian passions boil beneath it. As a child, he was subject to fits of anger. . . . While they lasted he did not know what he said or did."[19] Perhaps it was the years at Ham that taught him to veil such passions, for we rarely read of an angry outburst after 1848. Laughter, yes, but only in private. Then he could easily give way and laugh until near tears, often at his own jokes, which sometimes had a tinge of vulgarity. But he never talked very much, appearing distracted or dreamy.[20] His cousin Mathilde related an incident at Compiègne in 1863 when a servant with a seltzer bottle accidentally squirted him on the neck. He simply held out his glass on his other side and showed no anger. "If I had married him," Mathilde remarked, "it seems to me that I would have cracked open his head to see what there is inside!"[21] Early in the Second Empire, when we might suppose that he was still susceptible to public adulation, he was seen to be apparently unmoved by the cheers of a throng. Questioned about this coldness by the Comte de Tascher who accompanied him, he responded: "It is because I know men, Tascher."[22]

With self-control went tenacity of purpose. Lord Malmesbury, who became British foreign minister in

[19] Mme. Cornu to Senior, *op. cit.*, 599-600.

[20] Dr. Ernest Barthez de Marmorières, *The Empress Eugénie and Her Circle*, London: T. Fisher Unwin, 1912, p. 98.

[21] Edmond and Jules de Goncourt, *Journal*, Paris: Charpentier, 1893, II, 168.

[22] Tascher de la Pagerie, *op. cit.*, I, 25.

1852, had known Louis-Napoleon for over twenty years; he advised his ambassadors abroad that the new emperor would be a man of "obstinacy of intention, which, as it is maintained on all subjects with an unruffled temper, is held to the last against all opposition. All projects once formed and matured in his head remain there perfectly uncommunicated in detail, but their practical attempts or fulfilment will be a mere question of time."[23] To Lord Cowley, who would have the task of dealing with the emperor directly in Paris, Malmesbury added: "You may depend upon his being a man of action and counsel, relying on no other agent but his own inspirations, but with great self-command and power of self-denial if his passions are at variance with his interests. He is very superstitious, and was formerly very accessible to romantic and chivalrous impressions, and in private transactions most jealous of his *word* and his *honour*."[24] How shrewd these predictions were may be seen in the agonized reports home from ambassadors in Paris who groped for the threads of Napoleonic policy. Even during the Crimean War, when Britain and France were allies, Lord Cowley complained about the lack of French governmental policy, saying that there could be none because the foreign minister did not really know what the emperor was going to do next.[25]

The French foreign ministers and other officers of the crown also found this governing technique mystifying;

[23] Malmesbury, *op. cit.*, I, 324.

[24] *Ibid.*, I, 310-311.

[25] F. A. Wellesley, *The Paris Embassy during the Second Empire*, London: T. Butterworth, 1928, p. 30. From the papers of the first Earl Cowley.

sometimes, when uninstructed, they sought to develop policies of their own, only to be scolded for diverging from the emperor's policy, diverging in fact from the cause he represented. On May 24, 1859, Napoleon wrote these confidential words to Comte Walewski, then foreign minister: "If I do not represent the French Revolution in Europe, then I represent nothing at all, and it would be much better to have Henri V in my place, for the Revolution means the principles of '89." He carefully noted that the principles of '89 should not be confused with those of '93. After describing the constitutional structure of the Second Empire for Walewski, Napoleon concluded: "I go over all this with you, because it is very important that my ministers always be well imbued [with my] basic ideas, and I want you to reread the *Idées napoléoniennes* which I wrote in 1837 [*sic*]. My convictions are unchanged."[26] No doubt Napoleon laid down his basic policies in those pamphlets written before 1848, but the practical politicians of his day, knowing him to be a consummate politician, must be excused for assuming that his writings were mere propaganda and for failing to see him as a man of convictions. Beyond that, a minister could not be expected to know precisely how or when the emperor meant to implement his principles unless given unequivocal instructions.

We might expect that Napoleon's tenacity of purpose had been shattered by the humiliation of defeat in 1870. The Prussian General Graf Karl von Monts, who became Napoleon's jailer after Sedan, had shared the common view of the emperor as a man of corrupt and weak char-

[26] Comte d'Orano, *La Vie passionate du comte Walewski, fils de Napoléon*, Paris: Les Editions Comtales, 1953, p. 210.

acter, yet he knew that Napoleon had conducted himself bravely in the last battle, needlessly exposing himself to enemy fire in order to be killed. Monts once asked the emperor, therefore, why he had not committed suicide after failing to be killed. To die in battle would be to die honorably for his cause, Napoleon answered, but to commit suicide would have been an admission of hopelessness. He still had a mission, the one he had always had: the restoration of empire. He knew now that a restoration would necessarily be in favor of his son, but *that* he would work for.[27]

If anything, his celebrated self-control was greater in adversity than in prosperity. He was released by the Prussians in March of 1871 for an exile in England, and on his second day at Camden House in Chislehurst he was visited by his old friend Lord Malmesbury: "After a few minutes he came into the room alone, and with that remarkable smile which could light up his dark countenance he shook me heartily by the hand. I confess that I never was more moved. His quiet and calm dignity and absence of all nervousness and irritability were the grandest examples of human moral courage that the severest Stoic could have imagined."[28] On the day of Napoleon's death in 1873, the local priest told a newspaper correspondent that from the moment Napoleon had arrived in England he had never pronounced one bitter word against even his most unjust enemies.[29] Chislehurst never

[27] Henri Welschinger, "La Captivité de Napoléon III à Wilhelmshöhe (5 septembre 1870-mars 1871)," *Revue des deux mondes*, LVI (March-April 1910), 628.

[28] Malmesbury, *op. cit.*, II, 417.

[29] Francis Aubert, *Le Journal de Chislehurst, du 9 au 17 janvier 1873*, Paris: E. Lachaud, 1873, p. 11.

heard the fault-finding or the backbiting of St. Helena.

But then there was nothing of the harsh soldier-administrator about Napoleon III. Rather, with a softness, a generosity of spirit, a humanitarianism unknown in the first emperor, he was an un-Napoleonic Napoleon who could charm his friends and subjects but who sometimes lacked the rigor and toughness essential to leadership. To compare the two emperors' posthumous reputations, moreover, is to confirm Machiavelli's dictum that it is better to be feared than to be loved; for the one was remembered as the Great, the other as the Little. Both men were dictators, but Napoleon III lacked the autocratic spirit and gradually shed his dictatorial powers, perhaps for dynastic or opportunistic reasons, but in good faith, in good humor, and with grace.

Indeed, Sir William Fraser believed that Napoleon III's dominant character was his "good-nature," and Benjamin Disraeli believed he could trace Napoleon's errors and his eventual defeat in large part to his genuine kindhearted faith in the French people.[30] Napoleon III took great pride in his ancestors,[31] but his kind toleration of those Bonapartes alive in his time was the first proof of his generosity. Princess Mathilde was decidedly the best of the lot, but as a divorced woman she carried on an open liaison with the Comte de Nieuwerkerque. Her brother, Prince Jerome-Napoleon, was erratic and unreliable, an autocrat given to frequent radical pronouncements, a constant embarrassment to the regime. Their father, old King Jerome, spent considerable energy investigating Napoleon III's paternity, hoping to prove illegitimacy in order to

[30] Fraser, *op. cit.*, p. 176.

[31] Dr. Thomas W. Evans, *The Second French Empire*, New York: D. Appleton, 1905, pp. 31-65.

advance the claims of his own line. "You have nothing of the emperor in you," King Jerome shouted one day when refused money beyond his share from the civil list. "Alas," Napoleon replied, "I certainly have something in common with him: his family."[32]

Napoleon notoriously indulged the prince imperial, to the empress's annoyance, and she said that it was impossible to bring up a child properly with the emperor around. The child early learned that when he was forbidden something, he could get his way by speaking to papa about it. Called Loulou by the emperor, the prince was once caught trying to put a whole orange into his mouth. Alarmed, Napoleon asked Tascher to take the orange from the child, which was done despite his outcry. The emperor explained to Tascher that he himself could not have taken the orange from the child as "he would not then love me." It was a relief to all when the prince was put under the tutorship of General Frossard, who provided much-needed discipline. Even the emperor knew the need for it and did not interfere, delighted not to have to enforce it himself.[33]

After 1851 the emperor's half brother, the Comte de Morny, showed a lack of tact about his origins that was especially galling to the emperor, who treasured his mother's memory. Morny had portraits of both Queen Hortense and her lover, General Flahaut, in his salon and his carriages bore his arms, which included a blooming hortensia and a bend sinister. Yet the emperor could

[32] Dr. Prosper Ménière, *Mémoires anecdotiques sur les salons du Second Empire*, Paris: Plon-Nourrit, 1903, p. 31; and Count Horace de Viel Castel, *Memoirs*, London: Remington, 1888, I, 117.

[33] Bicknell, *op. cit.*, pp. 146-149.

not bring himself to complain to Morny about the display and finally asked the empress to do something about it. Her Majesty took up the matter with Morny, who said that he had thought the facts in the case were so well known that there could be no harm in making no attempt to hide them. Said the empress: "There is a great difference between something well known and something advertised."[34] The portrait of Hortense subsequently vanished from the Morny salon. In 1863 the emperor raised Morny to a dukedom and provided him with new arms that referred to Flahaut rather than to Hortense.

Members of Napoleon's household were continually struck by examples of his kindness. Tascher told of how he was once writing a letter in a private room when the emperor entered. He insisted that Tascher continue his writing, all the while pacing the room, smoking, humming a tune. When the letter was finished and sealed, the emperor said, "Have you finished, Tascher?" "Yes, Sire." "*Quite* finished?" "Yes, Sire." "Then I may take the inkstand?"[35]

Mocquart, the emperor's secretary, found it easy to work for His Majesty, partly because he was solicitous for those around him, partly because he had a habit of listening courteously to them. This led sometimes to softness and vacillation, but once he had made a decision he was not only firm but generally obstinate. Mocquart refused to write down his memoirs, because he knew that he would have to be silent about the very matters that would be most significant. Moreover, he believed that it

[34] Emile Ollivier, "La Mort de Morny et ses suites," *Revue des deux mondes*, 5th Period, IX (1902), 307.

[35] Bicknell, *op. cit.*, p. 49.

would be difficult to write a satisfactory account of that period of history from the sources to which historians usually turn, for those who knew the real causes of events were usually silent. No doubt this is true of all periods of history, but Mocquart, who worked so closely with the secretive emperor, was convinced that the historical problems relating to the Second Empire would be especially elusive.

Occasionally in conversation Mocquart would reveal bits of information, but they were always revealing of the emperor personally, not of matters of state or policy. He was one of the sources on the emperor's self-control, his resolution, his placidity, and his courage. Mocquart could tell precisely the disposition of the imperial mind according to the emperor's morning greeting. Sometimes it was "Bonjour, Mocquart," or "Bonjour, Monsieur Mocquart," or perhaps "Bonjour, Monsieur le comte de la Mocquardière." This set the tone for the day. As for the emperor's vacillation, Mocquart said that the coup d'état of 1851 had long been pondered, and that it was carried out only after three postponements. When a firm decision was finally made, Mocquart, the student of Tacitus, wrote *Rubicon* on the envelope that contained the plans.[36]

Perhaps Emile Ollivier, as a former member of the Republican opposition who rallied to the Liberal Empire and formed its first cabinet, was the most controversial of Napoleon's officers. Many Republicans, of course, regarded Ollivier's behavior as opportunism, though it has since been convincingly shown that throughout his career

[36] Dr. Ménière, *op. cit.*, pp. 441-443.

he was consistent in political principles.[37] Beyond the matter of principle, however, we may suspect that Ollivier was one of the many who were charmed by the emperor and became deeply devoted to him. Even defeat and disaster in 1870 did not alter Ollivier's sentiments, and he believed that a restoration was possible so long as the emperor lived. When Ollivier received word of the emperor's death, he wrote numerous letters expressing his grief and discouragement, including this eulogy: "His feelings were so lofty, so noble, so sensitive; how superior to the meanness of our era." In these letters Ollivier mourned a friend, not simply a sovereign.[38]

When Napoleon confiscated property belonging to the Orléans family in 1852, his action was seen as proof of a revengeful disposition.[39] Perhaps his motive was revenge against the dynasty that had imprisoned him—that has never been clear. But a fallen regime is an easy target, as the emperor himself would find after 1870, and he must also have been tempted to seize great wealth that could be used for charity and hence for political advantage. Whatever the motive, it was an impolitic move for a man widely held to be the defender of private property and order, and it raised doubts about the emperor's character. But this alone could not account for the durable tradition that held him to be a cruel and crass ruler. In his time and after, those who opposed him politically

[37] In Theodore Zeldin, *Emile Ollivier and the Liberal Empire of Napoleon III*, London: Oxford University Press, 1963.

[38] Emile Ollivier, *Lettres de l'exil, 1870-1874*, Paris: Hachette, 1921, pp. 151-161.

[39] Wellesley, *op. cit.*, p. 3.

accused him of operating a police state, and such a ruler is believed to be necessarily vicious. A refinement of this tradition developed among liberals during their commendable opposition to the Fascist dictatorships in our century. When they wrote history, they could not banish the contemporary dictators from their minds, and strong executives in earlier eras suffered in retrospect. Sometimes such historians saw Napoleon III as a forerunner of fascism, sometimes as the perfect political cynic, plotting successfully for power and interested in power alone.[40]

Subsequent scholarship has greatly modified such views, showing that the Second Empire did not vary substantially in censorship or in arbitrariness from those regimes that preceded and followed it.[41] As for political cynicism or indifference to the welfare of the governed, the charge is hardly tenable considering the emperor's well-known attempts to improve the conditions of life for his people. Many of them may have disagreed with him on one matter or another, but the results of the plebiscite of 1870, favoring him seven to one, proved that he still enjoyed the loyalty of the masses after twenty years of rule.[42]

What censorship and arbitrariness there was seems to

[40] For two examples of this tendency at home and abroad, see Marcel Emerit, *op. cit.*; and J. Salwyn Schapiro, *Liberalism and the Challenge of Fascism*, New York: McGraw-Hill, 1949.

[41] Note especially Irene Collins, *The Government and the Newspaper Press in France, 1814-1881*, London: Oxford University Press, 1959; and Howard C. Payne, *The Police State of Louis Napoleon Bonaparte 1851-1860*, Seattle: University of Washington Press, 1966.

[42] Georges Duveau, *La Vie ouvrière en France sous le Second Empire*, Paris: Gallimard, 1946, p. 56.

have been regretted more by the emperor than by his conservative entourage, the emperor always hoping to reconcile his opponents, his entourage convinced with some reason that the opposition was intransigent.[43] During the Crimean War, for instance, when many in the Republican opposition hoped for failure in the war to discredit the emperor, the radical Armand Barbès, in prison since 1849 for insurrection, wrote an impassioned letter to a friend: "A [military] success would in no wise strengthen this man if the people are against him. Defeats may kill us—France, I mean; and our dear country must live and be great and strong for the good of the world." The letter was intercepted by the police and shown to Napoleon, who ordered that Barbès be released unconditionally as a patriot.[44] Unable to decline the favor, Barbès chose to go into exile. After Orsini's famous attempt upon Napoleon's life in 1858, the judicial authorities were horrified that he might prevent Orsini's execution, for after receiving Orsini's petition exhorting him to champion Italian freedom, Napoleon said, "Orsini is not a common murderer like Pianori [another would-be assassin]. He is a man and has my respect."[45] Had not so many innocent people been killed in the Orsini attempt, Napoleon probably would have intervened. In any case, he did not demonstrate what Lord Cowley had called "a revengeful disposition."

Shortly after Edouard Thouvenel was removed from

[43] Gordon Wright, "The Distribution of French Parties in 1865: an Official Survey," *Journal of Modern History*, xv (Dec. 1943), 295-298.

[44] Octave Aubry, *The Second Empire*, New York: D. Appleton, 1940, p. 135.

[45] *Ibid.*, p. 194.

the foreign ministry in October of 1862, the emperor and an aide-de-camp were strolling in the Bois de Boulogne. A child rolled a hoop against His Majesty, who caught it and stooped to kiss the child while giving back the hoop. The child avoided the kiss, stating that his father had said that the emperor was a very bad man, and that he hated him. The emperor questioned the child as to his father's occupation and was told that the father did nothing at all: "He is a senator!" At this, the aide-de-camp was outraged and asked the child the father's name; but the emperor intervened saying, "la recherche de la paternité est interdite."[46] Because of the youth of the child and the advanced age of most senators, those who heard the story believed the child to be Thouvenel's son. If the emperor thought so too, we do not know; but he did nothing to prevent Thouvenel's election to the vice-presidency of the Senate somewhat later.

Inasmuch as most elections to the Académie française during the Second Empire favored men hostile to the empire, their formal reception by the emperor after their election was often tense; occasionally a new immortal would refuse to be received. Napoleon was keenly aware of this opposition but always refused to make these receptions the occasion for ill-temper or snubs. When Prévost-Paradol was received in March of 1866, the emperor began by expressing his regrets that a writer of such distinction was not one of his friends, to which Prévost-Paradol replied that he, too, was sorry. Then the emperor continued: "You did not share my views of Caesar in your [inaugural] speech, but our views coincide more in your

[46] Bicknell, *op. cit.*, pp. 165-166.

Universal History."[47] Paradol was astounded by this observation and wrote of the incident to his friend Halévy, who promptly looked up both versions of Caesar. In his speech Paradol had referred to Caesar as a tyrant. Twelve years before in the *Universal History*, he had seen Caesar as a great man. Perhaps Caesar had been both at once, but Napoleon had carried off the honors in his exchange with Paradol, who was left to be flattered that he had been read by the emperor.

Napoleon offered another writer, Leconte de Lisle, a pension of three hundred francs a month in 1870 on condition that he dedicate his translations from the Latin to the prince imperial. Leconte rejected the offer, saying that it would be a sacrilege to dedicate the masterpieces of antiquity to a child who could not understand them. He got the pension anyway.[48] Despite his kindness to these hostile authors, the emperor was in fact somewhat contemptuous of their opposition to the regime. "Literary geniuses," he said, "who meddle in politics should be sent to Colney Hatch."[49]

During Napoleon III's captivity after Sedan, the London *Times* hired a German journalist named Martin Cohn to interview the emperor at Wilhelmshöhe. Cohn, who wrote under the pseudonym of A. Mels, was impressed by the generosity of Napoleon's European views. He recalled his goal of a closer unity within Europe, calling the "transformations" in Italy and Germany the first steps toward producing the union of all European states

[47] Ludovic Halévy, *Carnets*, Paris: Calmann-Lévy, 1935, I, 92.

[48] F. L. Lucas, *Style*, New York: Collier-Macmillan, 1962, p. 58.

[49] Comtesse Louise de Mercy-Argenteau, *The Last Love of an Emperor*, London: Iris, 1916, p. 136.

into a single confederation. But Bismarck, complained Napoleon, belonged to a different school, preferring to revive the ancient hatreds separating the French and Germans, and using that hostility to subjugate the remaining German states. "The Napoleonic idea today has succumbed to [Bismarck's view], but history will judge which of the two was the more just, the more worthy for civilization and for humanity."[50]

The exile was, in other words, faithful to the Napoleonic idea, as he understood it, past the bitter end. To recognize this is to realize why Napoleon had not simply been a vulgar seeker after power for its sake alone. Though he was an enigma to his contemporaries because of his taciturnity and his secrecy, there was in contrast a simplicity about him in his unswerving devotion to his mission and in his quiet exercise of supreme power. The Goncourts, certainly indifferent to his regime, nevertheless understood this characteristic well in their journal entry of February 3, 1867: During a series of interviews with Emile Ollivier, Napoleon had asked Ollivier to speak quite frankly about what was being said in public about the emperor. Ollivier concluded his report by saying that the public found the emperor's faculties weakening. Said Napoleon, "That conforms to the reports I have received!" Added the Goncourts: "The response is quite like him, and in his impersonality he achieves a certain greatness."[51]

But there was nothing of the great warrior in him. On May 21, 1859, after the engagement at Montebello, the emperor visited the battlefield, his first experience of such

[50] Welschinger, *op. cit.*, pp. 912 and 920.

[51] Goncourt, *op. cit.*, III, 102.

a place. Never before had he seen the dead piled up, most of them horrible to see in their last contortions. He was taken to a field hospital, a large barn used as a vast operating room for both French and Austrian wounded. The emperor went in—to be choked by the odor of the place. Surgeons in aprons worked at kitchen tables, examining, cutting, and dressing wounds. In one corner he saw a pile of amputated hands and feet; he heard the shrieks and cries, the curses and groans. From this scene he was taken to a hospital in nearby Voghera where he passed along rows of litters, greeting doctors and chaplains.[52] Ten days later at Vercelli, the sight of dead and wounded again horrified him. He became silent, reflective, and seemed to hear nothing,[53] evidently overwhelmed by the pain of war. When in April of 1864 he offered his services to the committee in Geneva then preparing the Red Cross convention, he was responding to his agonizing experiences of 1859.[54]

His sensitivity extended also to animals. During the battle of Solferino, Dr. Larrey's horse was seriously wounded, losing much blood and visibly suffering. The emperor asked that the horse be removed from his sight. Larrey was able to stop the bleeding and had the weakened horse removed by placing it between two other horses so that it would not fall to left or right as it walked

[52] Germain Bapst, *Le Maréchal Canrobert. Souvenirs d'un siècle*, Paris: Plon, 1903-1904, III, 292-293.

[53] Général H. Bonnal, *Le Haut commandement français au début de chacune des guerres de 1859 et de 1870: étude sur la psychologie militaire de Napoléon III en 1859 . . . et de Bazaine en 1870*, Paris: R. Chapelot, 1905, p. 57.

[54] Victor Duruy, *Notes et Souvenirs*, Paris: Hachette, 1901, II, 119.

slowly away.[55] This incident recalls a famous bullfight held in Bayonne in September of 1856 when the imperial family was in residence at Biarritz. In those days the horses used in the arena were unpadded, and one bull alone killed twelve horses that day. From the moment the first horse was killed, the emperor lowered his eyes to his program and would raise them only when asked by his attendants to recognize the man who had to dispatch a bull. Four bulls were killed that day, but a fifth bull became frightened and refused to charge. Napoleon insisted that the animal be removed from the arena and spared.[56]

No aspect of the Napoleonic tradition was a greater liability for Napoleon III than that which required him to be a dashing and brilliant commander of armies. As a young man he had been an officer in the Swiss militia, and he had studied the campaigns of Napoleon I, especially in Adolphe Thiers's histories. As for notions of strategy, his ideas were those that any other nonprofessional could have developed from reading Baron Jomini's *Précis de l'art de la guerre*, published in 1837. During the Crimean War Napoleon had remained in Paris, as his British allies were fearful that his presence in the Crimea would win him much prestige and whet his appetite for conquest. What he did learn during that war is that bickering generals can jeopardize a campaign, and his decision to be generalissimo in both 1859 and 1870 may well have reflected a belief that only he could impose cooperation upon his subordinate generals. With his taste for technical innovation combined with his political skill he

[55] Archives du Musée du Val de Grâce, Carton 202.

[56] Fraser, *op. cit.*, p. 27; and Dr. Barthez, *La Famille Impériale*, p. 85.

might have been a splendid military administrator, but in 1859 he was utterly unprepared to be a commander in chief in the field. It became necessary for Marshal Vaillant, the minister of war, to fulfill many of the commander in chief's functions; as Vaillant, an engineering officer, was seventy years of age, obese, and unable to move on horseback faster than a walk, much of the work in fact fell upon his senior aide-de-camp, General Martimprey.

In preparing his strategy for the campaign of 1859, Napoleon asked for recommendations from his two most trusted generals, Niel and Frossard, both engineering officers, and from Adolphe Thiers. When he was dissatisfied with the plans that all three submitted, he asked Baron Jomini, then eighty years old, to offer a plan. Thus, Napoleon's liabilities as a commander in chief were threefold: He had to rely upon advice from a variety of sources, which contributed to great irresolution and an inability to act swiftly to counter Austrian moves; he could not enjoy the confidence of many of his subordinates who knew only too well that he was not a soldier; and he was so stricken by the sights of war that it necessarily affected his ability to plan and to act. It has reasonably been suggested that, in his concern for the loss of life, the emperor sought to avoid a decisive battle and hoped to win through successful maneuvering. The effect was to permit his enemy more time for preparation, to allow the Prussians time to mobilize and to threaten to intervene, and ultimately to produce heavier casualties when major battles were joined.[57]

Napoleon's political enemies found it easy, when the stories of his tenderness became known, to convert the

[57] Bonnal, *op. cit.*, pp. 15-47.

tenderness into cowardice. But the more reliable military witnesses said that the emperor never lost his sang-froid. At Magenta his hesitations were too lengthy because he appealed to too many officers for advice. On the other hand, once he had made up his mind he was very stubborn in realizing his ends, the very characteristic he showed in his political actions. On occasion, moreover, his decisions were bolder than those his generals counseled. When the army had landed at Genoa, for example, he ordered an immediate advance upon Piacenza despite his generals' warning that they were not ready to move. "On s'organisera en route," Napoleon replied, and they moved.[58]

After the Italian war he turned to scholarly aspects of war more suitable to his temperament. During his studies for his *Histoire de Jules César*, he discovered a modern use for Roman javelins and had a few of them constructed from his Roman models. He thought that they could be used in the physical training of soldiers to develop both strength and dexterity. He was, however, dissatisfied with the javelins made up for him and nothing came of the project, presumably to the relief of his military advisers.[59] As Tocqueville had written, Napoleon was by nature a dreamer and a visionary, sometimes able to cope with problems judiciously and with subtlety and depth. Yet there was "a little vein of madness running through his better sense."[60]

[58] *Ibid.*, pp. 98-103.

[59] Val de Grâce, Carton 109, General Castelnau to Dr. Larrey, November 13, 1860.

[60] Alexis de Tocqueville, *Recollections*, New York: Meridian, 1959, p. 227.

The quality of his mind baffled his contemporaries, partly because the madcap attempts upon the throne in 1836 and 1840 did not seem to square with the political shrewdness he exhibited after 1848, partly because he had deliberately cultivated impassive facial features. The long mustache was intended to conceal the expression of his mouth, and during conversation he would endeavor to keep his eyes expressionless, sometimes closing them entirely. Moreover, his speech had a slight German accent acquired in his youth, and his insensibility to French poetry when he delighted in Shakespeare, Goethe, and Schiller made his mind seem un-French to those who knew him well. He took pleasure in switching from French to German in conversation, a conversation that one visitor said resembled that of a German scholar more than that of a ruler of France.[61] A better than average scholar, he could read Latin well and knew some Greek, and he loved study and writing much more than conversation.[62] It was said of him that he knew five languages and could be silent in all of them.

His store of factual knowledge was not exceptional save in military matters, he was a deliberate thinker, and he tended to express himself simply and naturally, sometimes wittily, in a manner entirely free from officeholder's hokum. Yet Madame Cornu claimed that he had a penchant for the grand, the strange, the tragic; that a vigorous imagination was his predominant faculty (the vein of madness?), and that he ought to have been a poet. It is not well known that he delighted in hoaxes. We might

[61] Ernest II, Duke of Saxe-Coburg-Gotha, *Memoirs*, London: Remington, 1888-1890, III, 75.

[62] Mme. Cornu to Senior, *op. cit.*, pp. 601-602.

not expect that in a man who, when he wished to pay someone the supreme compliment, would say that he had "good sense." For he thought this to be the sovereign quality and the quality of a sovereign.[63] He never believed himself to be infallible[64] but was willing to confess his mistakes. Power, supposedly the corrupter of us all, seems to have had the opposite effect on the emperor's mind and judgment.

Madame Cornu's observations in this respect are especially significant. In the first place, she knew him better and longer than any other individual did, and she shared his liberal idealism. Consequently, she fell out with him after the coup d'état of 1851, thinking that he had betrayed the ideals of their youth. They were finally reconciled in March of 1863 when she became convinced that he still genuinely leaned toward liberalism, which she saw as the key to perpetuating the dynasty. Hortense Cornu was never blinded by his rank. Even at the time of the reconciliation, she knew that his governmental difficulties were increasing, and she was critical of his kindness to old political friends who were liabilities to his government. On the other hand, she believed that the emperor had grown in competence and insight, that power had actually improved him—in every respect, that is, except his weight, for he was getting less exercise than ever before and was becoming fat.[65]

As Napoleon himself recognized, he knew men. And because it was so obvious to others that he had insight, his

[63] Augustin Filon, *Memoirs of the Prince Imperial (1856-1879)*, London: William Heinemann, 1913, pp. 47-49.

[64] Ernest II, *op. cit.*, III, 76-77.

[65] Mme. Cornu to Senior, *op. cit.*, pp. 608-610.

failure to admit that some of his major officers were moral and political liabilities baffled observers. Lord Cowley put it well in a letter to Lord Clarendon on January 31, 1856: "I cannot help asking myself: is this shrewd, penetrating man really deceived, or is he trying to throw dust in my eyes? . . . There is an air of candour and honesty in his whole tone and manner that I would fain believe cannot cover deceit. Perhaps he has made up his mind that nothing can cleanse the Augean stable."[66] He also had to recruit support wherever he could, for republicans and royalists by and large would not serve him, at least not until the last years of the reign. He knew the inadequacy of mediocre politicians who surrounded him, just as he was aware of the mediocrity and the selfishness of most members of his family.[67] Political principles and idealism aside, one of the motives for liberalizing the regime in the eighteen-sixties was the aging emperor's search for more reliable supporters who could insure the succession of his son. From the beginning he knew that his name and popularity would suffice only temporarily to make the regime secure or permanent. This he revealed during his tour of the French countryside in 1852. A bishop in one of the towns he visited told him that he was adored in that locality, indeed, that many socialists had replaced Louis Blanc's picture in their homes with his portrait. "Do you really believe, Monseigneur," Napoleon answered, "that everyone who hangs a portrait of the Virgin in his home is a good Catholic?"[68]

[66] Sir Victor Wellesley and Robert Sencourt, eds., *Conversations with Napoleon III*, London: E. Benn, 1934, pp. 105-106.

[67] Emerit, *op. cit.*, pp. 145-146.

[68] Malmesbury, *op. cit.*, I, 358.

Those who knew Napoleon III always reported that his remarks were apt to be amusing. His wit had a facetiousness about it that veiled the seriousness behind a remark. Once when he was listening to the prince imperial read, the child stopped to ask a question: "Papa, what is the difference between an accident and a misfortune?" "Well, Louis," the emperor explained, "if our cousin [Jerome] Napoleon were to fall into the Seine, it would be an accident. If someone pulled him out, it would be a misfortune."[69] Another time when he was talking to Ernest II of Saxe-Coburg about the merit of uniting nationalities into self-governing states, the conversation turned to the Iberian peninsula. Napoleon wondered aloud about whether the decay of Spain and Portugal might be stemmed by uniting them into one state. When Ernest protested that their traditions of independence were too ancient to permit such a transaction, Napoleon ended the discussion by saying, "Well, you could tell the Spanish that you were giving them Portugal, and tell the Portuguese that you were giving them Spain."[70] Ernest was not amused.

Of the fine arts, the only one that interested Napoleon was architecture, probably Madame Cornu thought, because of the vastness of its products.[71] He knew nothing of music and had little interest in painting. He was said to have enjoyed the battle scenes of Horace Vernet and the animals of Rosa Bonheur, but little else. One evening at Biarritz, the conversation turned to a hunting scene

[69] Edward Legge, *The Empress Eugénie 1870-1910*, London & New York: Harper, 1910, p. 399.

[70] Ernest II, *op. cit.*, III, 61.

[71] Mme. Cornu to Senior, *op. cit.*, p. 598.

hanging in the Louvre, one canvas that Napoleon could identify: "Oh yes, I know which it is: a painting in which one sees nothing but masses of hunting dogs and hunting horns, and you cannot tell them apart as they are all *en trompette*!"[72] His inability to be a convincing patron of the arts was a significant disadvantage in Paris and one which his empress could do nothing to repair.

From an early age Napoleon, the heir to the tradition imparted to him by his mother, had believed that he was fated to rule France. His certainty of succession, however, went beyond his hereditary right or his conviction that the "Napoleonic idea" must ultimately triumph, for he was also a believer in astrological prophecies of his succession. And as such he was susceptible to the mysteries produced by spiritualists even during his reign. In 1857 a famous Scottish medium named Daniel Dunglas Home was a guest of the imperial family at Biarritz. Home's father had been an illegitimate son of the tenth Earl of Home; his mother came from a family noted for second sight. The mother took her son to the United States where she evidently schooled him in the family tradition, and when he returned to Britain in 1855 he soon acquired a reputation and many disciples. Home, only twenty-four when he appeared at Biarritz, affected a simple, awkward, timid air that especially displeased members of the medical staff, who thought that he was an accomplished master of duplicity. Furthermore, they worried over the possibility that the opposition would fall upon Home as the true source of imperial government. Actually, Home seems to have limited himself to simple tricks like table-turning and producing scratching noises, and once the

[72] Dr. Barthez, *La Famille Impériale*, pp. 81-82.

empress felt a tug on her gown. All this took place under a table where no one could look, feel, or examine.

Home was at least partly unmasked several weeks after his arrival when it was found that he wore very light slippers, easily cast off under the table. His socks had evidently been cut to leave his toes free, making it possible for him to tug at a dress, ring handbells, or give a few raps. The empress in her faith refused to accept this as evidence of fraud, but when Home was privately notified that he had been found out, he feigned a nervous attack and alleged that he was surrounded by spirits. He was further advised to stop such pretense.[73]

Napoleon told at least one of his friends that he had found his own horoscope, with its interpretation, in his mother's papers after her death. It prophesied not only his crown, but also that his reign would end disastrously. Thus he would say that this prior knowledge had helped him to prepare for adversity, and that in 1870 he had anticipated the Prussian victory. We would hardly give credit to such a story were it not for the fact that the emperor made other fatalistic remarks in 1870. Moreover, when that same friend visited him in his prison at Wilhelmshöhe in February of 1871 he told her that when he first arrived there he had been astonished to find a portrait of his mother on the wall. Or, as he put it, "my mother was here, waiting for me."[74] That incident was also reported by other witnesses.

Napoleon had reached the throne in 1852 as a forty-four-year-old bachelor, a serious lapse for a man who hoped to reestablish a dynasty. In the spring of 1836, it

[73] Dr. Barthez, *The Empress Eugénie*, pp. 137-141, 164-165.

[74] Mercy-Argenteau, *op. cit.*, pp. 182-190, 231.

had appeared that he might marry his cousin Mathilde, the daughter of King Jerome. Louis-Napoleon was then twenty-eight, she not yet eighteen. The possibility grew out of a visit Mathilde made to Queen Hortense that spring. King Jerome approved the match and wrote to King Louis in Florence to obtain his consent. King Louis's reaction might have been predicted: He did not think highly of marriages within the family and warned his son not to proceed. King Jerome, having no direct response from Louis, took Mathilde to Florence to visit him, where she found him a very tiresome and neurotic man. Evidently King Louis then gave way and promised his cooperation if the financial arrangements could be worked out. It was then discovered that King Jerome could not raise a satisfactory dowry for his daughter. By the end of August no arrangements had been made, and King Jerome went off to London to visit another brother, King Joseph.

This breakdown in negotiations was harder on Louis-Napoleon than on Mathilde, for he had real affection, perhaps love, for her, whereas she would recall that she felt a warm friendship for her cousin rather than true love. She had also been somewhat concerned that to marry him would sentence her to life at Arenenberg, a dull provincial existence, when she really aspired for a husband who could live in Paris. In October of that year the family got word of the Strasbourg fiasco, which infuriated them, and King Jerome forbade his daughter to write to either Louis-Napoleon or Queen Hortense.[75] It seems likely that Louis-Napoleon's decision to try for the

[75] Princess Mathilde Bonaparte, "Souvenirs des années d'exil," *Revue des deux mondes*, XLIII (January 1, 1928), 88-91.

French throne that fall was linked to this proposal of marriage, for if he did not secure position and money quickly, he would lose Mathilde for good. Indeed, in the spring of 1840 when he got word of Mathilde's engagement to Comte Demidoff, it spurred him to make plans for a new attempt on the throne, the landing at Boulogne on August 6.[76] No doubt Louis-Napoleon would in any case have made attempts to seize the throne, but the actual timing of the attempts reflected his determination to marry Mathilde. Years later many were to regret the failure of this match, as it would have likely been a better marriage than either of them had had, and Mathilde would have given his regime a semblance of cultural leadership.

In 1852 it became a matter of state that he marry, and the first negotiations toward that end were undertaken with Ludwig III, Grand Duke of Hesse-Darmstadt, for the hand of his daughter Caroline (whose mother was Louise, Princess Vasa). The suggestion for this marriage came from Napoleon's cousin Stephanie, the Dowager Grand Duchess of Baden (née Beauharnais). As Caroline was Stephanie's granddaughter, such a marriage would have linked the Bonaparte-Beauharnais clans more closely with a distinguished and royal family. The House of Vasa, even though it had been deposed in Sweden in 1809, was still regarded by most royalists as legitimate. The

[76] Comte E. C. Corti, "Correspondance du roi Louis et de Louis-Napoléon interceptée par la police de Metternich, 1833-1840 (première partie) Louis-Napoléon et son projet de mariage avec la princesse Mathilde," *Revue des études napoléoniennes*, XXVI (January-June 1926), 173-176; and (deuxième partie) "Les Complots de Louis-Napoléon et l'état d'âme de son père," *ibid.*, 248.

negotiations seemed to go favorably until the Hapsburg Dowager Archduchess Sophie intervened. Reputed to be Ludwig III's mistress, she had great influence over him, and she nourished a great hatred for the Bonapartes. Napoleon threw the faithful Tascher into the fray, but to no avail. Ludwig III ended the matter by announcing that as he had never renounced his right to the Swedish throne—his legitimate right—he would not compromise his claim by allowing an alliance with a chief of state who was not a member of a legitimate house.[77]

Morny was the architect of the second attempt to arrange a royal marriage. In this case the choice was Princess Adelaide of Hohenlohe-Langenbourg, daughter of Ernest, Prince of Hohenlohe-Langenbourg and Anne Frederika (née Saxe-Coburg-Gotha), thus a grand niece of Leopold I of Belgium and a second cousin of Ernest II of Saxe-Coburg. But the critical person in the decision was Queen Victoria, a half sister of Princess Adelaide's mother and highly antagonistic to Napoleon III after the confiscation of the Orléans properties. The French ambassador in London was instructed to try to overcome her antagonism, and Lord Malmesbury, then foreign minister, was urged to apply discreet pressure. The match was probably doomed from the outset, but when Napoleon invited the Montijo women for a week at Compiègne in December of 1852 he compromised his chances beyond repair. On January 11, 1853, the Prince of Hohenlohe-Langenbourg wrote a lengthy letter to the French ambassador in London to outline the reasons why such a marriage was unsuitable: The princess was Lutheran, she was

[77] Edmond Bapst, *Projets de mariage de Napoléon III*, Paris: A. Lahure, 1921, pp. 10-37.

only seventeen, she was not in good health, the family had recently lost another daughter to illness at the age of nineteen, and, finally, the princess herself felt unequal to the position. A few years later, when Victoria and Napoleon III were allies, the princess was to regret her lost opportunity.[78]

Napoleon had already foreseen the difficulties in making a royal match and in the autumn of 1852 had talked confidentially to his cousin Mathilde about the problem. She thought that he might make a beginning by abandoning his current mistress, the well-known Miss Howard. He admitted the tactfulness of such a move, but added that in her place he would want as a wife a beautiful woman whose lover he could be. This sounded ominous to Mathilde, who knew the rumors that he might choose the lovely Mademoiselle de Montijo, a Spanish aristocrat but not royal. In the absence of a wife, Mathilde had been acting as Napoleon's first lady, and she found it humiliating that she would have to give way to a woman not her social equal or superior. When it finally became clear that Eugénie de Montijo would be his choice, Mathilde preferred to think that he did not want to suffer any more refusals and made the choice in the knowledge of a sure acceptance. But she had reason to know that he wanted a wife who would be his mistress and not merely the mother of his heirs. In any event, the two women never liked each other, and Mathilde's persistent and public liaison with the Comte de Nieuwerkerque during the Second Empire became the accepted reason for her estrangement from the Tuileries, for the liaison could not be officially encouraged. Other than that, Napoleon, always

[78] *Ibid.*, pp. 39-82.

fond of Mathilde, would pardon her other indiscretions and her criticisms, as he knew that she was entirely loyal to him.[79]

Marie-Eugénie-Ignace-Augustine de Montijo was the daughter of Don Cipriano Guzman y Porto Carrero, a grandee of Spain; her mother was a daughter of William Kirkpatrick, American consul at Malaga and American by nationality, if Scottish by birth. Most of Napoleon's entourage were indifferent to his obvious infatuation with Eugénie's beauty and charm of manner and held out to the bitter end for a royal match. But on January 22, 1853, he announced before Parliament his engagement to the woman whom he loved and respected, predicting accurately that she would be the ornament of the throne and a courageous support in time of danger. When he added that she would bring the virtues of Josephine to the throne he was clearly unfair to Eugénie, but it was understood that he must think well of his grandmother. The marriage was celebrated at Notre Dame on January 30, 1853, and Napoleon took his bride to the palace, certain that he had married the woman who would be his mistress.

[79] Marguerite Castillon du Perron, *La Princesse Mathilde, un règne féminin sous le Second Empire*, Paris: Amiot-Dumont, 1953, pp. 124-128, 142.

> Women and governments who boast of their own virtue are both to be distrusted.
>
> Napoleon III

2 *The Curse of Love*

Napoleon III had always been fond of women, beginning with his mother, and he had been a prince with a great name. Before he came to the presidency in 1848 at the age of forty, he had had love affairs, perhaps like any other man. Reaching power, he became the victim of pamphleteers and an immense amount of gossip, the fate of any man in political office, no doubt, especially in France. But as a single man with a mistress who was no secret, political and personal factors combined to guarantee him a reputation as a sexual monster. Any woman who crossed the threshold of the Elysée Palace risked her reputation, and even the innocent pleasures there were popularly known as orgies. The eager acceptance of the chroniques scandaleuses as factual, and the human propensity to believe the worst about the great, have made the task of the historians of Napoleon difficult; not to speak of the fact that each one of them brought his own notion of sexual normality and propriety to the case. At best we are faced with a study in probability, for the mysterious nature of any individual's sexuality has in this instance been further clouded by malicious publicity. Finally, men of high rank, whatever their sexuality, are victims of ambitious women who seek to benefit from rumors that they are mistresses and hence have influence; or they can be victimized by women who seek to prove paternity in the hope of a financial settlement, whatever the truth of the situation.

The earliest of such charges seems to have been made by a woman in Switzerland named Knussy, who alleged that she had been born to a common woman in either 1822 or 1823, and that Prince Louis-Napoleon had been her father.[1] He would have been fourteen or fifteen at the time of her birth. Even most of the scandalmongers have treated that charge as dubious. Some writers, however, have said that a Mrs. Gordon was his mistress in 1836 at the time of the Strasbourg attempt. She was born Eléonora-Marie Brault in 1808, her father an officer in the imperial guard. She married Sir Gordon Archer, but evidently also became the mistress of Persigny and shared his enthusiastic Bonapartism. Known as Madame Gor-

[1] Mitarra, "La descendance naturelle de Napoléon III," *La Vie judiciaire*, #365 (1953), p. 9.

don, or Mrs. Gordon, when she was widowed in 1836, she was used by Persigny to attract the assistance of Colonel C.-N. Vaudrey, who commanded the 4th Regiment of Artillery at Strasbourg. Rumors associated her as well with Louis-Napoleon. She was captured with the other Strasbourg plotters, tried in 1837, and acquitted.[2]

Only between 1840 and 1846, when Louis-Napoleon was at Ham, do we find satisfactory evidence of his amours. His laundress, Alexandrine Eléonore Vergeot, bore him two sons. As she later married a man named Bure, both children were given his name. The elder was Alexandre-Louis-Eugène, born February 25, 1843; the younger was Alexandre-Louis-Ernest, born March 18, 1845. Bure himself, during the Second Empire, was given a minor bureaucratic post in the imperial household. As for the two boys, an imperial decree of June 11, 1870, created the elder Comte d'Orx, the younger Comte de Labenne, the titles themselves being created to represent new estates in the reclaimed areas of Les Landes. Both men served briefly in the bureaucracy of the Second Empire, Labenne dying without heir in 1882, Orx living until 1910.[3]

Two more sons were attributed to Louis-Napoleon at Ham, but in these cases the evidence is doubtful. General Montholon, Louis-Napoleon's companion in prison, had a mistress named O'Hara whom he later married. She gave birth on April 1, 1843, to Charles-Jean-Tristan de Montholon, who later served in the French foreign service

[2] Hector Fleishmann, *Napoleon III and the Women He Loved*, London: Holden & Hardingham, 1915, pp. 30-54.

[3] Ernest Alfred Vizetelly, *Court Life of the Second French Empire*, New York: Charles Scribner's Sons, 1907, p. 184.

and died in 1899 without heirs. His paternity, however, has been attributed to Louis-Napoleon on the grounds that it was not likely that Montholon, then sixty years of age, could have become a father.[4] There is no more reason to accept such a supposition than there is to believe that Léon Massé, the son of a jailer's daughter at Ham,[5] was Louis-Napoleon's child. Not only is the evidence lacking, but there were no titles created for these men.

The maîtresse en titre during those years was, in fact, the well-known Miss Howard. Louis-Napoleon had met her in England before the events that led to Ham, she visited him there, and she retained her position during his presidential years. On August 16, 1842, she gave birth to Martin-Constantin Haryett, and it has been logically assumed by many that Louis-Napoleon was the father, especially since he created Haryett Comte de Béchêvet in 1865. It is well established now that Major Mountjoy Martyn was the actual father, and Haryett's creation was more a gesture of regard to the then discarded Miss Howard than an admission of responsibility.[6] Besides Miss Howard during the presidential years, a long run of actresses supposedly had access to the president; but we are forced to doubt the validity of much of the gossip.[7] The separation between Louis-Napoleon and Miss Howard was painful for both of them but made necessary by his impending marriage. A separation contract, signed in 1852, provided her with title and income, and she tried to fulfill her responsibilities under the contract by seeking

[4] Adrien Dansette, *Les Amours de Napoléon III*, Paris: Fayard, 1938, p. 75.

[5] Mitarra, *op. cit.*, p. 9.

[6] Vizetelly, *op. cit.*, p. 183.

[7] Fleishmann, *op. cit.*, pp. 115-119.

an English husband. Finally, in mid-1854, she married Clarence Trelawny, the second son of a great landed proprietor.[8]

By the standards of his day for a man of his rank, Louis-Napoleon's love affairs before his marriage were "moderately respectable."[9] If one objects to that judgment by insisting that the illegitimate children born at Ham amounted to infidelity to Miss Howard, his loyal mistress, it can be pointed out that she could visit him only infrequently and that he had, after all, been sentenced to life imprisonment. By 1853 his condition was altered in two major ways: He was now an emperor, and the demands upon him meant that he needed unusual physical and emotional consolation. Second, having surrendered a mistress of over a dozen years, he found himself wedded to a totally unresponsive woman, something he had never before experienced. What followed may have been unfortunate, but it was a predictable performance for a normal man.

Under the best of circumstances a couple may prove to be incompatible. The imperial marriage was initially constrained by the publicity of palace life, and the couple had none of the privacy of a honeymoon so often necessary for a good adjustment. The gap between their ages was significant if not insurmountable, approximately eighteen years, but the difference in sexual experience was more serious.[10] Not only had Eugénie had none, but she

[8] Simone André Maurois, *Miss Howard and the Emperor*, New York: Alfred Knopf, 1957, p. 114.

[9] T.A.B. Corley, *Democratic Despot, A Life of Napoleon III*, London: Barrie & Rockliff, 1961, p. 143.

[10] Simone Maurois, *op. cit.*, pp. 104-105.

had a profound ignorance of a husband's needs that even the passing years did not remedy. His infidelities began after about six months of marriage. In every other respect he was a perfect husband, and she never had any doubt that he loved her.[11] On the other hand, the "conjugal affronts"[12] that she began to experience were mortifying, especially since she could really not understand their reason. Her conception of a wife's role was only too clearly revealed in 1865 at a time when the imperial family was promoting the marriage of Anna Murat to Lord Granville, which Anna was resisting: "Tell her," the empress said to Walewski, "that after the first night it makes no difference whether the man is handsome or ugly. By the end of a week it's the same old thing."[13] And she attributed the emperor's infidelities not to his sensual needs but to the monotony of his imperial situation of which she was a part. She brought him nothing new or fresh: "So, man roams!"[14] She did, however, manage to produce an heir to the throne. But after the birth of the prince imperial on March 16, 1856, which nearly killed the empress, her physicians told her that another pregnancy probably would be fatal. This became the excuse to deny the emperor further sexual relations. As she put it to her old friend Prosper Mérimée, "there is now no longer any

[11] Augustin Filon, *Recollections of the Empress Eugénie*, London & New York: Cassell, 1920, p. 35; and Dansette, *op. cit.*, p. 185.

[12] Mme. Carette, *Recollections of the Court of the Tuileries*, New York: D. Appleton, 1890, pp. 63-64.

[13] F. A. Wellesley, ed., *The Paris Embassy during the Second Empire*, London: T. Butterworth, 1928, p. 275.

[14] Filon, *op. cit.*, pp. 34-35.

Ugénie [Napoleon's pronunciation of her name]. There is only the empress."[15]

Her recovery from the confinement was slow and accompanied by noticeable depression that lasted longer than is usual after pregnancy. In her worst moments she sought comfort from her sister Paca, the Duchess of Alba, who without question was the person with whom she was most intimate.[16] In a letter to Paca on December 31, 1857, though the words referred to insults she had received as empress, Eugénie's disenchantment with marriage is also obvious: "I have such a disgust for life, things past seem so empty, the present so full of obstacles, and the future perhaps so short (at least I hope so), that I often wonder to myself if it is worth the struggle, and courage fails me."[17] Their correspondence reflects an essential sisterhood to which Eugénie had retreated in dismay. On September 16, 1860, Paca succumbed to a spinal disease while the imperial couple were on a state visit to Algeria. Napoleon felt obliged, because of their official duties, to conceal the news temporarily from Eugénie. When she learned the truth, she was not only grief-stricken but furious at him for the deception. Her hysterical behavior, which included a mad trip incognito to Scotland and irrational fears that she shared Paca's fatal disease,[18] was attributed at the time to her resentment at Napoleon's infidelities, triggered by this last deception.

[15] Simone Maurois, *op. cit.*, pp. 127-128.

[16] Mme. Carette, *op. cit.*, pp. 64-65.

[17] Duke of Alba, ed., *Lettres familières de l'Impératrice Eugénie*, Paris: Le Divan, 1935, I, 143.

[18] Harold Kurtz, *The Empress Eugénie 1826-1920*, London: Hamish Hamilton, 1964, pp. 153-160.

In fact she had lost the adult dearest to her, and in the coming decade she would emerge as a grief-matured woman, as Madame Carette put it, devoted to the future of her infant son and willing to engage in politics toward that end.

Meanwhile, the frustrated emperor had begun looking elsewhere for consolation. His first thought was for Miss Howard, whose loss he much regretted and who had been anticipating his return. After about six months of marriage, that is, in the late summer of 1853, he did return to her. In September the empress warned him that she would leave him if he did not break completely with Miss Howard. He had no choice but to comply.[19] Subsequent gossip encompassed a bevy of singers and actresses, much of it catalogued for historians by Comte Horace de Viel-Castel, who had an ear for scandal and the temperament of a wasp. Most of those who have quoted him have also cautioned against his prejudices and probable unreliability, thus perpetuating his tittle-tattle without incurring responsibility.

Viel-Castel, however, was no simpleton. His literary style reveals a subtle and inventive mind, and he was second in command at the Louvre to Comte Nieuwerkerque, embittered in his knowledge that he was abler than his superior. Even so, his position in the artistic world gave him access to intellectual and literary circles, most of them hostile to the empire. The gossip he passed on was at the time attributed to Princess Mathilde. Yet those who really knew her knew that she did not tolerate remarks reflecting on the imperial house in her presence, and there must be considerable doubt that she would have passed

[19] Simone Maurois, *op. cit.*, pp. 112-113.

on to Viel-Castel the variety of intimate information he peddled.[20] No doubt some of what he said and wrote was true, but with his taste for the scurrilous and his access to a ready market for it, we shall probably never know how much he embroidered and fabricated. The Goncourt brothers also recorded titbits for posterity, no doubt less maliciously than Viel-Castel, but with a fascination with the bizarre and the dreadful that left them often uncritical of their sources. For instance, on March 15, 1862, they rushed home to record in their *Journal* that "when a woman is brought to the Tuileries, she is undressed in one room, then goes nude into another room where the emperor, also nude, awaits her. [The Chamberlain,] who is in charge, gives her the following instruction: 'You may kiss His Majesty everywhere, except on the face.'" Amusing perhaps, but does it have the ring of truth?

Since the emperor's premarital affairs with Vergeot and Howard were common knowledge, Eugénie must have been aware of them before she decided to marry him; probably, recognizing his infatuation, she felt confident that her great beauty would suffice to hold him, and she could have had no foreknowledge of her frigidity. Despite her subsequent disgust with sex, the birth of the prince imperial in early 1856 was at least proof that sexual relations continued into 1855. In those years, however, the emperor's health began to deteriorate, and what evidence remains points to the marital discord as one source of his decline. They were also the years of the Crimean War, which gave him more than his share of anxieties. The empress was worried about his state and

[20] Vizetelly, *op. cit.*, p. 194.

attributed it to the worry and misery the war had caused him.[21]

The emperor and his senior physician, Dr. Conneau, finally decided to call in Dr. Robert Ferguson of London for consultation.[22] Dr. Conneau had been a faithful and trustworthy friend, but Napoleon must have had some qualms about Conneau's medical credentials (of which more later), and the choice of a foreign physician suggests an unusual desire for secrecy. On May 6, 1856, Ferguson, having completed his examination of the emperor, read his case-report to the emperor in the presence of Dr. Conneau. His general verdict was nervous exhaustion. The symptoms he noted were varied and numerous, but he pointed out that His Majesty's inability to sustain his usual amount of exercise and his fatigue after any effort were in strong contrast with his vigorous, well-nourished frame. He thought that there had been no damage to the brain, rather that the brain had become "irritable." Thus, His Majesty, having been a good sleeper, was now easily disturbed, and once disturbed he remained wakeful. Even after undisturbed sleep the emperor awoke unrefreshed, recovering from that state only late in the day.

He was also experiencing occasional intense pain in the cutaneous nerves in various places. Sometimes the pain persisted only a few minutes, sometimes for two

[21] Wellesley, *op. cit.*, p. 101.

[22] Not to be confused with Sir William Fergusson, his more famous contemporary who held the chair of surgery at King's College Hospital. British officials who learned of the consultation simply spoke of "Dr. Ferguson," and subsequent historians inferred that it must have been Sir William despite the difference in spelling. The actual case-report is written in Ferguson's hand and is also signed by him.

days. It had been relieved, but never cured, by external applications of anodynes or irritants. Ferguson noted also a slight tendency to spasmodic contraction of the fingers of both hands accompanied by a sensation described by the emperor as one of "pulling or drawing." The fingers, including the joints, seemed somewhat swollen. Otherwise, the motor nerves seemed in no way impaired.

The emperor also complained of loss of appetite. Even after an appetizer or a glass of wine, his stomach became uncomfortable after small quantities of food. His bowels were irregular, sometimes constipated, and he had used cathartics. The bowels were sometimes painful, seemingly hard and distended, but Ferguson could locate no painful spot or pressure. He was told that the emperor had hemorrhoids, dating from his imprisonment at Ham, but that they had ceased to bleed ten years before.[23]

Not included in the original case-report, by consent of His Majesty, was a description of another malady that may well have been the primary motive in seeking the consultation. The emperor discussed it privately with Ferguson and again in the presence of Dr. Conneau. Recently he had been experiencing a loss of sexual desire and potency. Not only had sexual intercourse become rare, but after it he remained wakeful for the rest of the night, whereas previously he had found that it contributed to his sound sleep.[24]

Some of Dr. Ferguson's negative findings were also important for the emperor's medical history. He found nothing unnatural about the heart and lungs, there had

[23] Dr. Robert Ferguson, Case-Report of May 6, 1856, Library of the Royal College of Physicians, London.

[24] *Ibid.*, Case-Report annex, May 9, 1856.

been no hepatic pain or jaundice, and there was no enlargement of the liver. He found nothing abnormal in the renal secretion: no deposits, no trace of albumin or sugar. But since the specific gravity was a bit low (1012), he advised that the urine should be analyzed from time to time. Finding no evidence of any structural disease, he thought that the emperor's condition had been produced simply by overwork and the absence of his usual exercise, affecting the nervous and the digestive systems in particular. Though he was told that, many years before, the emperor had been given doses of mercury, Ferguson did not think either mercury or any other drug had been responsible for the excessive sensitivity of the skin or the cramps.

Ferguson's prescription, accordingly, was fairly simple. He advised a hot shower bath every morning on rising, followed by a rubdown, and protection of the skin in cold weather with flannel. He added that he believed smoking to be injurious, at least the heavy smoking of the emperor. As for diet, it should be as simple and light as possible, preferably only two meals, with the heavier one at midday. He might have fish or soup, followed by meat with a little vegetable and bread. One or two glasses of wine were permitted, but no fruit or pastry. As the emperor was little interested in food, the diet can have been no hardship for him. Ferguson recommended only mild cathartics so as not to exhaust the emperor unnecessarily. Evidently Dr. Conneau had already been giving the emperor an "alkaline mixture" which Ferguson thought should be continued only so long as any acidity in the urine remained. He also strongly recommended the use of thermal springs, mentioning no spa by name but saying that the waters should be soothing and slightly tonic.[25]

When Ferguson last visited the emperor on May 6 to read his report and make his prescription, he found him unusually pale, thoroughly exhausted, and suffering from a headache. Again in the presence of Dr. Conneau, Napoleon told Dr. Ferguson what had happened during the night, something that had also occurred two months before. He was awakened by a feeling of great pain and oppression in his chest, and found himself confused, frightened, and trembling—a condition that lasted nearly two hours. He also discovered that he had unknowingly wet the bed. Ferguson's response was to reiterate how necessary it was for the emperor to get as much relief from intellectual work as possible. Evidently this revelation struck Ferguson as much more serious than anything that had appeared in his actual examination, and to Dr. Conneau in private he said that it sounded like an imperfect epileptoid state, that it was possible that the nervous system was already dangerously disorganized, and that Napoleon might be on the verge of becoming an epileptic. He warned Conneau that he would see great changes in the emperor within five years unless the malady were arrested.[26]

Back in London Ferguson gave a further report of his examination to the Comte de Persigny, an old associate of Napoleon's and then French ambassador to Britain. Ferguson's excuse for this indiscretion was that Persigny had often expressed his concern for the emperor's health; also, perhaps he thought that if another close associate of

[25] *Ibid.*, Case-Report of May 6, 1856.

[26] *Ibid.*, Case-Report annex, May 9, 1856.

Napoleon's knew that the situation was curable, but potentially serious if not conscientiously treated, the emperor was more likely to get the necessary care. Ferguson did not give Persigny the more lurid details of the examination and avoided being specific. "I consider His Majesty," he concluded, "to have had his warning in the existence of the minor grades of suffering incidental to a formidable disease, and I would urge His Majesty's advisers to remove what I verily believe to be *now* remediable."[27]

Dr. Ferguson, moreover, evidently believed it to be his patriotic duty to inform the foreign minister, Lord Clarendon, of the emperor's state; he must have given Clarendon a more pessimistic report than he had given Persigny. For Clarendon at once wrote to Lord Cowley in Paris to anticipate great alterations in the emperor's character: "Apathy, irritation, caprice, infirmity of purpose are upon the cards, as the result of an exhausted nervous system and diseased organs, which ensue from such exhaustion. The political results of this may be fearful and we may soon have to make great allowances for physical infirmity."[28] Perhaps Clarendon drew more drastic conclusions than Ferguson intended, or perhaps Dr. Ferguson had professional doubts about the quality of the French medical service. In any case, British foreign policy framers were furnished alarming information about the future of Anglo-French relations.

Napoleon, meanwhile, was seeking a different form of therapy for what ailed him. He had already seen the magnificently beautiful Virginia, Countess of Castiglione at the end of 1855 when she had arrived in Paris, sent

[27] *Ibid.*, Case-Report annex, May 17, 1856.

[28] Wellesley, *op. cit.*, pp. 95-96.

there by Cavour to influence the emperor during the Congress of Paris. Like every other man he had been dazzled by her beauty. Sympathetic as the emperor already was with Italian nationalism, there is little reason to believe that the presence of the countess had anything to do with promoting the war of 1859 against Austria. On the other hand, there can be little doubt that by 1857 he was having an affair with the divine countess. But divine only in physical beauty, for she was without wit, without charm, of limited intelligence, and a notorious egoist. The precise duration of their affair is impossible to trace, though it was fairly brief, as was the case of all her subsequent affairs: She was incapable of any real affection or loyalty, and it was a matter of pride to have possessed her, little else. She joined the imperial court by invitation at Compiègne in 1857; in her will, she would ask to be buried in "the Compiègne nightgown, 1857."[29] Cash and fabulous jewels were her reward, and some suspected that her estranged husband also received compensation. Said the Count of Castiglione to Morny, "I am a model husband. I see nothing and hear nothing." "Yes," answered Morny, "*mais vous touchez*."[30]

During the liaison, the Countess of Castiglione occupied a house in Auteuil, and it is reasonable to credit reports that the prefect of police, Pierre-Marie Piétri, was distressed by orders not to post guards in that neighborhood in any way that might call attention to the emperor's nocturnal visits. Piétri was responsible for His Majesty's security, and he feared attempts on the emperor's life.

[29] Roger L. Williams, *Gaslight and Shadow: The World of Napoleon III*, New York: Macmillan, 1957, p. 149.

[30] Archives de la Préfecture de Police, Dossier B a/1002.

Whether he ultimately solved his dilemma by telling the empress of the danger is far from certain, but one version of the tale would have it that the empress then made such a scene with the emperor that he promised not to go out again at night.[31]

A better-known story, however, is more open to question because of the unreliability of the sources. Supposedly, an attempt at assassination *was* made at the Castiglione home, but the assassin was intercepted within the house by a police agent named Griscelli and killed with a knife.[32] The intent of this story was to implicate the empress, for the intended victim was presumably not the emperor but the Countess of Castiglione, her rival. The assassin was alleged to have been another police agent in the empress's pay.[33] Griscelli was indeed a police agent between 1851 and 1858, when he was dismissed from the service. But he was a known swindler with many years in prison to his credit, and after his expulsion from French territory in 1859 he served various masters and associated himself with anyone wishing to discredit the Bonapartes. One sample of his style should suffice: On March 4, 1879, shortly before the death of the prince imperial in Africa, Griscelli wrote to the prefect of police seeking reemployment and offering to publish a new brochure that would kill forever the party of "Napoleon the Last" by proving that the "fake warrior of Natal is a

[31] *Vingt Ans de Police, Souvenirs et anecdotes d'un ancien officier de paix*, Paris: E. Dentu, 1881, pp. 36-38.

[32] Jacques-François Griscelli de Vezzani, *Mémoires*, Geneva, Brussels, and London: n.p., 1867, pp. 111-113.

[33] *Mémoires de Monsieur Claude*, Paris: Jules Rouff, 1881-1882, I, 131-132.

bastard of the creature of Sedan!"[34] As for the *Memoirs of Monsieur Claude*, Claude was indeed chief of the Service de Sûreté from June 1, 1859, to July 10, 1875,[35] but the memoirs published after his death were spurious, written by an unknown but clever polemicist. One of the author's objects was to show that Napoleon III's mistresses were foreign agents—traitors—hence linking his escapades with the defeat of 1870.

Accordingly, it is safer to attribute the rupture between Napoleon and the Countess of Castiglione to the course of politics rather than to a shocking incident in Auteuil. For in 1859, aggrieved like many other Italians that Venetia remained Austrian, she became publicly critical of Napoleon's settlement of the war against Austria. Her words were possibly a signal that the liaison had already ended, but in any case they won her expulsion from France in 1860. She was allowed to return in 1861, by which time she had already begun the series of affairs that brought anguish to numerous men.[36]

Until recently it was believed that the Countess of Castiglione had borne Napoleon a son later known as Dr. Arthur Hugenschmidt. The child, actually born in 1862 to the wife of a palace majordomo, benefited from the emperor's kindness. The emperor urged his American dentist, Dr. Thomas Evans, to supervise the child's education and thus incurred suspicion of the child's paternity. Evans did help young Arthur, who ultimately com-

[34] Police Dossier, E a/113.

[35] Gustave Macé, *La Police parisienne. La Service de la Sûreté*, Paris: Charpentier, 1884, p. 142.

[36] Williams, *op. cit.*, pp. 150-158.

pleted his medical and dental degrees at the University of Pennsylvania. Returning to Paris to practice dentistry, Hugenschmidt began to repay the late emperor by asserting himself to be his illegitimate son and recalling the prince imperial as his playmate.[37] Moreover, he had a penchant for the mystical and found through spiritualism that his mother had been the Countess of Castiglione. He also cultivated the rumor that he had visited the widowed Eugénie in Farnborough after the death of the prince imperial and that she had been startled by his close resemblance to her late husband.[38] He in fact in no way resembled Napoleon, being especially tall, as a friend later testified,[39] and the best that can be said about Dr. Hugenschmidt is that he never fell victim to his own hoax. He died unmarried and childless in 1929, the Institut Pasteur being his chief heir, and in his will he admitted to being simply the son of Hugenschmidt, palace majordomo.[40]

Tradition has it, too, that Napoleon developed a second liaison in 1857, one that was more durable than his affair with the Countess of Castiglione, though similiar in the Italian beauty of the woman. She was Marie Anne de Ricci, who had become the wife of Comte Alexandre Walewski in 1846, thus ending his famous liaison with

[37] Dr. W. S. Davenport, Jr., "The Pioneer American Dentists in France and their Successors," *Revue d'histoire de l'art dentaire*, III, #7 (1965), 106-108.

[38] Dansette, *op. cit.*, p. 282.

[39] Dr. R. Benard, "Bâtards de Napoléon III," *Chercheurs et Curieux*, IV, #39 (1954), 288.

[40] Alain Decaux, *La Castiglione, dame de coeur de l'Europe*, Paris: Amiot-Dupont, 1953, pp. 324-326.

the actress Rachel. The new Madame Walewska, though a Florentine, also had Polish blood through her mother, who was a grandniece of Stanislas Poniatowski.[41] During the Second Empire it was generally assumed that she had taken Napoleon as a lover in order to advance her husband's career. Prosper Mérimée put it this way: "I do not know if it is true, as she claims, that her family originates with Machiavelli; what is certain is that *she* is descended from him."[42] Historians who have accepted this tradition have also accepted Viel-Castel as a reliable collector of scandalous stories; Viel-Castel, with his remarkable knowledge of extramarital details, was able to date the liaison from September 14, 1857.[43]

Beyond the gossip there were a few facts that pointed to a liaison. Comte Walewski's financial resources were limited, and in 1858 Napoleon ceded to him a property in Les Landes to provide more income. At the time, Walewski was foreign minister and no doubt needed private funds to maintain his establishment, but the gift was seen as a compensation to a cuckold. Second, it is a matter of record that the emperor was fond of Madame Walewska and showed her marks of affection in public. But this did not prove what Mrs. Trelawny (the former Miss Howard) bitterly believed, that "each reigning Bonaparte must sleep with a Walewska."[44] Upon Walewski's death in 1868, Napoleon repurchased the estate in

[41] Philippe Poirson, *Walewski, fils de Napoléon*, Paris: Editions Balzac, 1943, p. 126.

[42] Simone Maurois, *op. cit.*, p. 130.

[43] Alain Decaux, *Amours Second Empire*, Paris: Hachette, 1958, p. 63; and Fleishmann, *op. cit.*, pp. 198-200.

[44] Simone Maurois, *op. cit.*, p. 131.

Les Landes from the widow, giving her some ready money in exchange for the property, which had turned out to be rather unproductive. Walewski had, in fact, left her with very little else; after the fall of the empire, bank drafts in her name were found drawn on His Majesty's account at Barings of London. They proved nothing but fed the gossip. Finally, in 1869, the emperor provided her with an annual pension of 20,000 francs from his civil list, a gesture typical of his generosity.

Despite all this, the Empress Eugénie was not jealous at the time, and the two women continued to be good friends after the emperor's death in 1873. Yet Eugénie had been outraged by the Castiglione affair and would be shortly again by another. One historian has proposed that she tolerated this particular liaison, because it suited her pro-Papal politics to keep the pro-Papal Walewski in the foreign ministry.[45] It is an ingenious notion, if entirely alien to Her Majesty's character. The gossip of the day implied that Walewski himself tolerated the liaison to keep his high position secure, which, his best biographer assures us, was also foreign to his character.[46]

Madame Walewska's nephew, talking to his aunt in her old age and having access to the family papers, concluded that though Napoleon had delighted in her company he never made her his mistress. Perhaps the nephew was merely protecting the memory of his aunt, but he evidently knew in some detail the charges and countercharges and thought that the evidence was on the side of virtue. Much of the gossip, after all, came from the anti-Walewski factions, and they included Viel-Castel and

[45] Dansette, *op. cit.*, p. 237.

[46] Poirson, *op. cit.*, pp. 255-257.

Mérimée. Anticlericals much disliked Walewski's Catholic politics, his diplomatic abilities were widely believed to be limited, and he lacked the charm to win over doubters. Furthermore, Madame Walewska was already thirty-four when she became a regular member of the court and there were many younger and prettier women about. She had had three children, she was in an advanced state of pregnancy at that moment, and she was subsequently to suffer several miscarriages. Because many of the younger women were irritated by the emperor's indifference to them, they gossiped viciously about anyone who enjoyed his affection. She was, furthermore, a devout practitioner of a religion that forbade adultery, and after Walewski's death she would marry a man whose mistress she had steadfastly refused to become.[47] The case has to rest there, but she seems to have been acquitted.

Not so Marguerite Bellanger, who appeared on the imperial scene in 1863. If the details of this liaison have never been clear, that it took place cannot be doubted. She was born Julie Leboeuf in a small village near Saumur, where she was initially trained as a dressmaker.[48] But when she came to Paris, it was as a circus rider; once there, she attempted to convert that talent into a theatrical career, but was a total failure. Meanwhile, she had changed her name to Marguerite Bellanger in order to put an end to crude jokes, and had located near the École Militaire to be available to the army officers in that neighborhood. They called her Margot. Somehow she got from the Boulevard La Motte-Picquet to Saint-Cloud, probably

[47] Comte d'Orano, *La Vie passionante du comte Walewski, fils de Napoléon*, Paris: Les Editions Comtales, 1953, pp. 238-243.

[48] Police Dossier B a/957.

as the companion of an army officer taking part in an imperial hunt, and there the emperor saw her. He established her in the rue des Vignes, where she reigned for nearly two years.[49]

Her presence was not long a secret from the empress. For one thing, Marguerite lived ostentatiously on the money the emperor provided (though she would later say that she had been interested less in the money than in the title "mistress to Caesar"), and Napoleon himself was responsible for some publicity, because he allowed her to accompany him when he was away from Paris. On a trip to take the waters at Vichy, for instance, it was remarked that the baths seemed to tire His Majesty inordinately. The secretary Mocquart laughed and said that the emperor's amours had something to do with it.[50] Dr. Philippe Ricord, the specialist in venereal disease who was famous for his certainty that almost everyone would sooner or later require treatment, remarked: "If the emperor wishes to continue the Life of Caesar, he must cease being Pompey."[51] In an interview given in Belgium after the fall of the empire, Marguerite told of accompanying the emperor to the camp at Châlons for military maneuvers, and said that as a joke she had once entered headquarters dressed as a colonel of hussars. The emperor had told her that the empress, informed of the incident, had made a

[49] Louis Sonolet, *La Vie parisienne sous le Second Empire*, Paris: Payot, 1929, pp. 193-194; and Frédéric Loliée, *The Gilded Beauties of the Second Empire*, New York: Brentano, 1910, pp. 277-287.

[50] Dr. Pariset, "Quelques notes sur les cures de Napoléon III à Vichy," *la Chronique médicale*, XVII (April 1, 1910), 209-213.

[51] Désiré Lacroix, Letter to *la Chronique médicale*, XVII (August 15, 1910), 560.

terrible scene and had threatened to refer the marital situation to the papacy, and that it would be necessary to break off their romance.[52] Her reminiscences at that point were highly fictionalized and contributed considerable confusion to the case, so that no one can be sure which parts of her testimony were truthful.

She made no mention, for instance, of the astounding visit she unexpectedly received from the empress in 1864. Her Majesty forced Mocquart to take her to Marguerite's home, whereupon the empress told Marguerite that she was killing the emperor and that she must give him up. Marguerite stood her ground saying, "If you want the emperor not to come here, keep him at home with your charm, amiability, good humor, and gentleness. He comes here because you bore him and tire him." Poor Mocquart, at that time in delicate health and easily upset (he was to die on December 12, 1864), was so shocked by the conversation that he rushed from the room in tears. But when he returned he found the two women seated together and talking in a friendly manner.[53]

On February 24, 1864, several months before Eugénie's dramatic descent, Marguerite had given birth to a boy, henceforth called Charles Leboeuf. She told the emperor that the child was his, but Napoleon was convinced that he had not been responsible for it. Though almost everyone at the time and since has believed that he was, the emperor refused to provide a title for this child—who grew into an unusually tall young man, probably prov-

[52] Police Dossier B a/957.

[53] Marcel Blanchard, ed., "Journal de Michel Chevalier (1856-1869)," *Revue des deux mondes*, series 8, XII (November 1, 1932), 180.

ing the emperor's point.[54] The liaison was finished (she returned to military service),[55] but the question of the child lingered to harass the imperial couple. Among the papers found in the Tuileries after the fall of the empire were two which pertained to the child's paternity. Evidently the empress had asked Adrien Devienne, then first president of the Cour de Cassation, to offer Marguerite money if she would leave Paris, and Devienne also secured a written confession from Marguerite that the child was not Napoleon's.[56] Devienne was professionally compromised by this intervention when it came to light, but successfully defended himself by showing that he acted to prevent a probable separation of the imperial couple if the matter could not be legally closed.[57] Marguerite later stated that Devienne had threatened to have her put away in an insane asylum if she refused to sign the desired papers,[58] but the chances are that she would not have accepted the offered settlement had she believed that the child was really the emperor's. That Devienne was restored to the high court after 1871 further suggests that the legal inquiry into his intervention truly absolved him of having obtained a false confession.

Marguerite Bellanger was the last maîtresse en titre in Napoleon III's life, but not the last woman. That honor belonged to the Comtesse Louise de Mercy-Argenteau, born a princess of the house of Caraman-Chimay in 1837.

[54] Erwan Marec, "Un fils de Napoléon III à Lorient," *Les Cahiers de l'Iroise* (Brest) (new series), XIV, #41 (1967), 255.

[55] Police Dossier B a/957.

[56] *Papiers secrets et correspondance du Second Empire*, 3rd ed., Paris: Auguste Ghio, 1873, p. 34.

[57] Vizetelly, *op. cit.*, pp. 203-205.

[58] Police Dossier B a/957.

She was part of the older nobility that had avoided Napoleon's court, leaving the way clear for the contentious upstarts of dubious reputation who did his name no good. Over the years, however, she grew to admire his achievements and believed that he was always respectful of women. She did not meet him until she took part in a charity bazaar, November 18, 1866, in the Elysée gardens, by which time she was a curiosity because of the suicide of the Count of Stackelberg, whom she had refused to take as a lover. Napoleon was struck immediately by her blonde beauty (the empress, the Countess of Castiglione, and Marguerite Bellanger were all blondes), and by 1867 she was widely regarded as the emperor's "friend." In 1869 the Duc de Persigny sold her a home in the rue de l'Elysée, which gave her easy access to a private room behind the chapel in the Elysée Palace, and she came to suspect that Persigny, an old enemy of the Empress Eugénie, had offered her the house in the hope that she would serve to counter the empress's political influence.

In fact, the Comtesse de Mercy-Argenteau was then little interested in influencing imperial policies, and though she was to claim that she had been the emperor's last love, she added that she had not been his mistress.[59] Other factors in the emperor's life, as we shall see, give substantial support to her claim. The two met frequently in their private room, chatting amiably, and we may recall Marguerite Bellanger's assertion in 1864 that the emperor sought feminine companionship that did not tire or bore him. She was not only a dear friend, but one who remained loyal to the end, visiting him at Wilhelmshöhe

[59] Comtesse Louise de Mercy-Argenteau, *The Last Love of an Emperor*, London: Iris, 1916, pp. 33, 50, 60, 116-132.

when he was a German prisoner and rather foolishly intriguing against Bismarck in the aftermath of the war.[60]

In May of 1869 Baron Casimir Dudevant wrote to Napoleon applying for a decoration. He based his claim not only on his father's governmental service between 1792 and 1815 and on his own service since 1815, but also on his matrimonial history, which he thought would win the emperor's sympathy: "In the evening of my life," he noted, "I am anxious to receive the Cross of the Legion of Honor. Married to Lucile Dupin, known to the literary world under the name of George Sand, I have been cruelly denied the affection owed to a husband and a father. And I believe that I merit the sympathetic attention of all those who have known about the distressing events that have characterized that part of my life."[61] Probably Baron Dudevant, who did not receive the decoration, never knew that Napoleon kept a copy of the letter for many weeks on his desk and showed it to friends. But we may be sure that the letter received a friendly understanding from its recipient.

[60] Vizetelly, *op. cit.*, p. 373.

[61] The letter was found by André Maurois when he was working on a biography of George Sand (*Lélia*). The original can be found in the files of the Chancery of the Legion of Honor, a copy in the Spoelberch de Lovenjoul Collection: Group E.868, f.291.

One must fulfill one's [medical] obligations, not merely because law and propriety require it, but because of a love of virtue.
Baron Dominque Larrey

3 *The Imperial Medical Service*

The health service of the imperial household was created by the decree of December 31, 1852, but actually organized by Dr. Henri Conneau (1803-1877), the long-time friend of Napoleon III.[1] Conneau, who took the title of senior physician and chief of the health service, was born of French parents in Milan during the French occupation, his father being an officer in the commissariat.[2]

[1] Dr. A. Corlieu, *La Mort des rois de France depuis François Ier*, Paris: Honoré Champion, 1892, p. 323.

[2] R. Scott Stevenson, *Famous Illnesses in History*, London: Eyre & Spottiswoode, 1962, p. 94.

Conneau took his medical training in the Medical College of Florence, supporting himself for a time while still a student by being secretary to King Louis Bonaparte, then in exile. He abandoned his position in order to take practical training in a Florentine hospital, then received his medical degree on May 17, 1827. He practiced in Rome for the next three years until forced to leave for having treated some of the revolutionaries conspiring against the papal regime. In the process he became acquainted with King Louis's sons, who were among the conspirators, and this acquaintance led to an invitation to visit Arenenberg in Switzerland, where in 1831 he became the private physician to Queen Hortense.

Dr. Conneau remained with Hortense until her death in 1837, and thus was not one of Louis-Napoleon's Strasbourg conspirators in 1836. One of Hortense's last requests was that Conneau watch over her surviving son, a task he would perform faithfully until Napoleon's death in 1873. Napoleon's last words, in fact, would be for Conneau.[3] After the coup d'état of 1851, Conneau supported his master by running for a seat in the Corps législatif in the March elections of 1852 and became the deputy for the Third Constituency of la Somme.[4] (The fortress of Ham was in la Somme.)

Corsican in appearance, quite short, with a head and nose too large for his body, Conneau was usually smiling, and his dark eyes were full of mischief. Perhaps his most engaging quality was that he made no pretense of being

[3] Police Dossier B a/1.017; and Marcel de Baillehache, *Grands Bonapartistes*, Paris: Charles Tallandier, 1899, pp. 312-315.

[4] Archives Nationales, Carton C.1339, #191. He got 22,622 votes out of 32,422 registered voters, 23,189 actually voting.

an accomplished physician. He knew that his training had not been first-rate and that what he had learned was rusty by 1853. He was really the emperor's most intimate confidant, and with the organization of the medical household Conneau became more of a medical administrator than a practicing physician,[5] bringing to the service of the court doctors who were abler than he. In February of 1853 when the Académie de médecine met to fill four places vacated by death, his was the only name put forward, and he was unanimously elected by the seventy members present.[6] He was obviously a political rather than a medical choice. On August 12 of the same year Napoleon named him to be an officer of the Legion of Honor, and he was promoted to be grand officer on August 9, 1867.[7]

As of January 1, 1853, Dr. Conneau's salary was fixed at 30,000 francs a year; but on occasion he received from the emperor additional sums which were neither explained nor dated in the imperial records, in one case 8000 francs and another time 10,000 francs.[8] Since it has long been known that the emperor employed Conneau for secret missions involving Italian politics, it is entirely possible that these sums represented compensation for diplomatic expenses. The regular physicians and surgeons on Conneau's staff, four in number, were each paid 8000 francs a year; the eight consultants were retained at 6000 francs annually. The household list also

[5] Général Comte Carl de Monts, *La Captivité de Napoléon en Allemagne*, Paris: Pierre Lafitte, 1910, pp. 59-61.

[6] Archives Nationales, F17-3683. Election of Feb. 15, 1853.

[7] Archives Nationales, O[5] 120, the Conneau dossier.

[8] Archives Nationales, O[5] 80.

included eight more doctors who lived in different Parisian districts, who received an annual salary of 6000 francs, and who were responsible for the treatment of household employees. In addition to these twenty physicians and surgeons, an obstetrician (Dr. Paul Dubois, 1795-1871) was available for the empress and was the man who delivered her of the prince imperial in 1856, at which time Dr. Ernest Barthez de Marmorières (1811-1891) was appointed as pediatrician. Finally, the staff included as dental surgeon Dr. Thomas W. Evans (1823-1897), formerly of Philadelphia.[9]

Information about the men who made up the staff is quite uneven and fragmentary. But by piecing it together we can obtain an estimate of the medical skill available to the emperor as well as some notion of his attitude toward medicine. Moreover, even then medicine had its politics, and careers could be advanced or retarded for reasons other than medical ones. Take the case of Dr. Pierre-François-Olive Rayer (1793-1867), who was one of the initial regular physicians on the household staff. Known primarily as a specialist in skin and kidney diseases, Rayer had already treated Napoleon during his presidential years. Because of his eminence, Rayer was able to take the initiative in 1858 in establishing a special medical association for the Paris region and a general medical society for all France.[10]

In 1862, however, Rayer found himself in trouble when

[9] Albert Verly, *De Notre-Dame au Zululand*, Paris: Paul Ollendorff, 1896, pp. 105-106; Corlieu, *op. cit.*, p. 323; and Armand Dayot, *Le Second Empire*, Paris: Ernest Flammarion, n.d., p. 342.

[10] Bibliothèque Nationale, Nouvelles Acquisitions Françaises 5888.

the government acted upon a recommendation from Dr. Emile Littré (1801-1881) that two new chairs be created at the École de médecine. Littré was a famous intellectual and a physician, though never a practicing one; the translator of the works of Hippocrates in ten volumes; and the co-editor (with Dr. Charles Robin, 1821-1885) of the *Dictionnaire de médecine*—in which we find the celebrated definition of man that so infuriated Bishop Dupanloup: "Animal mammifère de l'ordre des primates, famille des bimanes." Littré's word carried great weight in the medical world, but unfortunately his recommendation came through the ministry of public instruction. One of the new chairs, in comparative medicine, created for Rayer because he had long carried on the comparative study of human and animal diseases, carried with it the deanship of the École de médecine. The faculty was indignant that the initiative had apparently come from the state, and intellectuals generally (and Ernest Renan in particular) opposed the reform. The medical students took the hint and greeted Rayer's maiden address with a great tumult, but he stood his ground and read every word of it. For the next two years he was unable to give a single lecture and finally resigned his post on January 18, 1864. Napoleon III tried to soften the blow by naming him a grand officer of the Legion of Honor, but his health quickly gave way. He died in 1867.[11] He was a learned man and a fine practitioner whose earlier career had been obstructed because of his Protestant origins, and

[11] Dr. Raoul Caveribert, *La Vie et l'oeuvre de Rayer (1793-1867)* (a medical thesis), Paris: Marcel Vigné, 1931.

his end was a sad loss to the imperial staff and to French medicine.[12]

Dr. Gabriel Andral (1797-1876) was another distinguished physician appointed as a regular member of the initial household staff. Under the July Monarchy he had already been a leading clinician in France, really a specialist in pathology; he was elected to the medical and surgical section of the Académie des sciences on April 11, 1843.[13] Perhaps less celebrated than his contemporary, Rayer, Dr. Andral managed to keep clear of political reprisals for his association with the emperor, maintaining his position until 1870.

A third initial appointment as a regular member of the staff was that of the surgeon Antoine-Joseph Jobert de Lamballe (1799-1867), who had previously been a consultant to King Louis-Philippe. Elected to the Académie de médecine in 1840, he became the first French surgeon to try a general anaesthesia, using ether in 1846. His election to the Académie des sciences did not come until 1856, at which time he was on the medical faculty of the University of Paris. During an operation in 1859 to remove a tumor from a woman who had an undiagnosed case of syphilis, Dr. Jobert accidentally infected himself and was unaware until too late of the source of his symptoms of decline. By 1865 he was totally mad and had long since ceased to be active on the imperial staff.[14]

[12] Dr. Maurice Genty, "Rayer (Pierre-François-Olive) 1793-1867," *Les Biographies médicales*, v (November 1931), 33-48.

[13] Archives Nationales, F17-3378.

[14] Dr. Maurice Genty, "Jobert (de Lamballe) Antoine-Joseph 1802-1867," *Les Biographies médicales*, v (October 1931), 17-32.

Dr. Baron Félix-Hippolyte Larrey (1808-1895) was the fourth initial appointee to the regular staff. The son of Dominique Larrey, chief surgeon for the Grand Army of Napoleon I, he was destined from the start for a career in military medicine, and his faith in Bonapartism had been as carefully nurtured by the elder Larrey as Louis Napoleon's own faith had been by his mother. "Without doubt," wrote father to son, "the most important [of all virtues] is the probity that characterizes the *honnête homme*, a title you want to deserve and one that I hope you achieve, for the notion is dear to my heart. Besides, always remember, my dear friend, that this title was sanctified in your papa by the greatest man who ever lived, so that after my death it ought to be the device on your arms."[15] The young Larrey began his medical training in 1828 at the military hospital of the Val-de-Grâce, which had been founded by decree of the Convention in 1793, using the confiscated buildings of the old Abbaye Royale du Val-de-Grâce de Notre Dame de la Crêche.[16] At the same time he enlisted in the army's Corps de Santé.

All the while he began to cultivate a career in Bonapartism by collecting books and memorabilia of the First Empire. Knowing of Queen Hortense's serious illness in 1837, he sought to find a suitable doctor who could go to Switzerland to aid Conneau in her care, and after her death he hoped to collect materials about her for an even-

[15] Bibliothèque Nationale, Nouvelles Acquisitions Françaises, 14478, letter of June 21, 1825.

[16] A. Mignon, *École du Val-de-Grâce 1852-1914*, Paris: Val-de-Grâce, 1914, p. 6.

tual biography,[17] a biography he never wrote. The elder Larrey died in 1842, and Dr. Larrey discovered in his possessions a portrait of King Louis Bonaparte by Gros. He sent it to Dr. Conneau at Ham with instructions that it should be presented to Louis-Napoleon as a measure of his loyal sentiments.[18] This was not crass opportunism but true cultism, the sincere expression of his paternal tradition, as he would put it in 1856 when congratulating the emperor on the birth of the prince imperial.[19] Even after the collapse of the Second Empire, Larrey remained a true believer, successfully running for a seat in the Chamber of Deputies as a Bonapartist in 1877 and publishing a book on Madame Mère in 1892.

In any case, his career had not depended on his Bonapartism, for he had advanced rapidly under the July Monarchy and was appointed to the Legion of Honor as a chevalier on April 25, 1845.[20] In 1850 he was elected to the chair of surgical pathology of the Académie de médecine in a contest with the brilliant Dr. Nélaton.[21] So that by the time he was appointed to a regular post in the imperial household, Dr. Larrey was well established in French medicine. His military medical rank (médecin principal de première classe) was the equivalent of colo-

[17] Bibliothèque Nationale, N.A.F., 5888, Baron Larrey to the Maréchale Ney Princesse de la Moskowa, Feb. 25, 1837; and Larrey to Mlle. Masuyer, Nov. 29, 1837.

[18] Bibliothèque Nationale, *ibid.*, Larrey to Conneau, Nov. 8, 1845.

[19] *Ibid.*, Larrey to Napoleon III, March 26, 1856.

[20] Val-de-Grâce, Carton 202.

[21] Archives Nationales, F17-3584.

nel, and he had been named the assistant director of the new École imperiale de médecine (1852) established in conjunction with the old hospital at the Val-de-Grâce. Although he was available for service at the Tuileries, it was understood that Baron Larrey's responsibilities for the emperor's health would be largely limited to times when the emperor attended military maneuvers or when he commanded in time of war. Beginning in 1857, annual maneuvers were held at the Camp de Châlons, generally in August or early September, during which time Larrey would be part of the imperial suite. Napoleon liked him and had him promoted to médecin-inspecteur (brigadier general) in 1858. The following year he served as chief physician for the army during the Italian campaign, after which Napoleon promoted him to be a commander in the Legion of Honor. During the Franco-Prussian War his military administrative duties were so great that he could not go to the front with the emperor, and Adolphe Thiers overlooked the Bonapartist loyalty to promote Larrey to grand officer in the Legion of Honor in 1871. He retired from active service on September 28, 1872.[22]

The unfortunate fates of Doctors Jobert and Rayer meant that the regular medical staff had to be augmented. The first to be added was Dr. Baron Lucien Corvisart (1824-1882), who had already been one of the household physicians employed to care for palace personnel from the time the medical household had been established at the very end of 1852. Like Baron Larrey, Baron Corvisart bore a great medical name dating from the First Empire.

[22] Val-de-Grâce, Cartons 109 and 202; and Dr. L.-J.-B. Bérenger-Féraud, *Le Baron Hippolyte Larrey*, Paris: Fayard frères, 1899, pp. 54-61.

For he was the nephew of Jean-Nicolas Corvisart, senior physician to Napoleon I. Lucien Corvisart was a scholarly man of science, well regarded by his contemporaries in medicine, and was primarily interested in the digestive system, in the pancreas, and in diabetes.[23] His appointment as a regular physician to Napoleon III was dated December 16, 1859.[24]

In the meantime, Dr. Conneau was beset by rising medical costs that, by 1859, made his budget for doctors and medicines seriously inadequate and increased his administrative headaches. One result was an imperial decree limiting free medication to personnel whose annual salaries were under 2000 francs; when that did not solve the financial crisis, the minister of the imperial household was forced, by the end of 1865, to augment the medical budget substantially.[25] Another change took place on November 1, 1866, when Baron Corvisart was promoted to be deputy physician to Dr. Conneau, so that his salary was raised from 8000 to 15,000 francs.[26] Whether this reflected the increase in administrative duties or Conneau's need for more professional support after Rayer's decline is unknown, but the latter seems more likely since it coincided with an obvious deterioration of the emperor's health. Corvisart had proved himself to be a loyal Bonapartist whose professional discretion could be counted on—and who would prove himself anew after the disaster of 1870.[27]

With Corvisart's promotion came a further appoint-

[23] Paul Ganière, *Corvisart, médecin de Napoléon*, Paris: Flammarion, 1951, p. 252.

[24] Archives Nationales, O^5 120.

[25] *Ibid.*, O^5 98.

[26] *Ibid.*, O^5 120.

[27] Police Dossier B a/1.019.

ment to the regular staff, that of Dr. Auguste Nélaton (1807-1873), the man defeated in 1850 by Dr. Larrey for a chair at the Académie de médecine. Nélaton had, however, won a place in the surgical pathology section on December 16, 1856,[28] and since 1851 he had been a professor of surgery on the University of Paris faculty. His distinguished clientele so absorbed his time that, upon the addition of the emperor in 1867, he resigned his teaching post for private practice. He was elected to the Académie des sciences that year, appointed to the Senate by the emperor, and created grand officer of the Legion of Honor.[29] Lectures he had given between 1844 and 1860, published together as the *Eléments de pathologie chirurgicale*, became a text for students of surgery on both sides of the Atlantic, and in 1863 he invented a flexible rubber catheter for use in probing patients afflicted with urinary or bladder problems, which was a marked improvement over previous instruments. Called the leading French surgeon of his day,[30] he also had his failings and failures, as we shall see.

The staff of consultants, eight strong, included men who were as distinguished in their time as the regular physicians and surgeons, though perhaps less well known to us. Dr. Alfred-Armand-Louis-Marie Velpeau (1795-1867), one of the initial consultants, was an outstanding surgeon specializing in problems of childbirth and female disorders, known as a fine clinician and teacher. He was

[28] Archives Nationales, F17-3684.

[29] *Ibid.*, O[5] 120.

[30] Dr. S. F. Marwood, "Louis-Napoleon and his Doctors," *Medical Journal of the Southwest* (Bristol), LXXXII (January 1967), 75.

elected to the Académie de médecine in 1832, to the Académie des sciences in 1842.[31] Dr. Louis-Jacques Bégin (1793-1859) was a military surgeon who taught in the hospital at the Val-de-Grâce. Though he was a member of the Académie de médecine, his candidacy for the Académie des sciences was narrowly defeated in 1858, a check that was fatal to his health. Dr. Pierre Honoré Bérard (1797-1858), a physiologist and surgeon, was a member of the medical faculty of the University of Paris, whose dean he was during the Second Republic, at which time he was also elected to the Académie de médecine. Dr. Charles-Emmanuel-Simon Gaultier de Claubry (1785-1855) was a physician particularly noted for his interest in immunization. A fifth man, Dr. Pierre-Charles-Alexandre Louis (1787-1872), a physician who retired in 1854, was a well-known participant in the controversies about the nature of tuberculosis.[32]

The three remaining initial appointments went to friends of Baron Larrey, suggesting that Dr. Conneau may have leaned heavily on Larrey's advice when establishing the medical household. One of them was the surgeon Baron Jules-Germain Cloquet (1790-1883). He had been a student of Dr. Achille Flaubert of Rouen and in 1857 was a great defender of his son, Gustave Flaubert. Dr. Cloquet had a special interest in urinary diseases, and when he began preparing to retire from a highly successful private practice, he sent his collection of calculi removed from patients to the museum of the Val-de-

[31] Dr. Maurice Genty, "Velpeau (Marie) 1795-1867," *Les Biographies médicales*, v (April and May 1931), 357-384.

[32] Corlieu, *op. cit.*, p. 323.

Grâce.[33] Baron Larrey responded by recommending that Dr. Cloquet be made a commander in the Legion of Honor.[34]

A physician in the military service, Dr. Michel Lévy (1809-1872) was the second friend of Larrey's appointed to be a consultant.[35] Beginning in 1836 he was the senior physician at the Val-de-Grâce, and he reached the rank of médecin-inspecteur (brigadier general) at the beginning of 1851. Lévy was chief of the medical corps that served in the Crimean War, and was primarily interested in infectious and contagious diseases—really a public health specialist. He became the second director of the new École imperiale de médecine in 1856 and held the post until his death in 1872. A religious man, he rejected positivism and the materialism characteristic of so many nineteenth-century physicians.[36]

The remaining initial appointment went to Dr. Jean Bouillaud (1796-1881). As a young man he had been an enthusiast for Rousseau, and in 1815 he had interrupted his medical studies to join a regiment of hussars to aid Napoleon I in his return from Elba. He kept politically active as a liberal after the Restoration, and it is likely that he became a Carbonaro for a time. Ultimately he was better known as a specialist on rheumatism and heart

[33] Bibliothèque Nationale, Nouvelles Acquisitions Françaises, 5888, Larrey to Cloquet, Jan. 25, 1856.

[34] *Ibid.*, 5889, Larrey to Conneau, July 23, 1860. Also see Dr. Maurice Genty, "Cloquet (Jules-Germain) 1790-1883," *Les Biographies médicales*, VII (January 1933), 261-273.

[35] Bibliothèque Nationale, Nouvelles Acquisitions Françaises, 5888, Larrey to Lévy, July 8, 1850.

[36] Val-de-Grâce, Carton 209/1, dossier 991.

disease, and their coincidence. Larrey and he had in common a devotion to the "Prometheus of St. Helena,"[37] and that no doubt aided Bouillaud in obtaining a nomination to be commander in the Legion of Honor from Napoleon III. He was elected to the Académie des sciences on June 1, 1868.[38] So well-known was he in his lifetime that he was consulted all over Europe, and we can still find him as Balzac's Dr. Bianchon in *Cousin Bette*. He was also the model for the Dr. Bouillaud who treated Renée Mauperin in the Goncourts' novel of that name.[39]

Five of the original consultants either died or retired before the end of the Second Empire and had to be replaced. Aside from Dr. G.-Maxime Vernois (1809-1877), whose career seems obscure, the replacements were well-known doctors. Dr. Ambroise-Auguste Tardieu (1818-1879), for instance, a professor of forensic medicine since 1861, was also a specialist in nervous disorders; it was he who was elected to succeed Rayer as dean of the École de médecine in 1864.[40] Dr. Pierre-Charles Huguier (1804-1873), elected to the Académie de médecine in 1848, was a surgeon appointed to the staff.[41] One of the last additions was Dr. Antoine-Sulpice Fauvel (1813-1884), a specialist on cholera who had lived in Turkey and taught medicine in Constantinople. Upon his return to France he was elected to the public health section of

[37] Bibliothèque Nationale, Nouvelles Acquisitions Françaises, 5888, Larrey to Bouillaud, Nov. 4, 1844.

[38] Archives Nationales, F17-3579.

[39] Dr. Henri-Georges Dejeant, *La Vie et l'oeuvre de Bouillaud*, Paris: Louis Arnette, 1930, pp. 11-22, 45-64.

[40] Dr. René Semelaigne, *Les Pionniers de la psychiatrie française avant et après Pinel*, Paris: J. B. Baillière, 1932, II, 50.

[41] Archives Nationales, F17-3684.

the Académie de médecine on April 13, 1869.[42] And, finally, the internationally famous Dr. Philippe Ricord (1800-1889), Baltimore-born and known through his published papers and letters. He was a venereologist, especially interested in syphilis, an interest from which perhaps derived his celebrated cynicism. His failure to diagnose Sainte-Beuve's bladder stones in 1867 (there were three of them), which were revealed through an autopsy in 1869,[43] was also well known.

Napoleon III had available to him, in sum, the best that French medicine could supply, but that in itself could not guarantee that he would in fact receive the caliber of care that was so immediately available. In the twentieth century we take it for granted that people of high political or social rank command and obtain the best that medicine can provide and that when the doctor prescribes the patient obeys, no matter how powerful he may be. The attitude of patients and doctors, especially surgeons, a hundred years ago was very different. Before the democratization of Western society and the remarkable advances in medical science, which combined to produce the attitudes we know today, surgeons were timid when forced to prescribe for people of high rank. The elder Baron Corvisart had always advised Napoleon I, when ill, to go to a military hospital, where he would be treated the same as any lieutenant or captain would be, rather than to be treated at the Tuileries where the fear of responsibility paralyzed the intelligence of the imperial doc-

[42] *Ibid.*

[43] Dr. J. C. Lemaire, "Des Médecins sous le second empire, #2 des chirugiens," *Bulletin interne des Amis de Napoléon III*, #8 (December 1968), 9

tors. Further, Corvisart *père* thought that a good doctor had to be more than intelligent: he had to be bold. In his opinion, the older the physician became, the more skillful in equivocation he grew, so that great experience became an actual liability.[44] Moreover, a staff of consultants deliberating as a committee, such as Napoleon III would have in 1870, could be paralyzed by conflicting views. Later on Léon Gambetta, suffering from appendicitis, remarked that if he were a simple worker he would be taken at once to a hospital, operated on, and possibly cured. Instead, a decision was postponed, and he died of a ruptured appendix.[45]

To make matters worse, Napoleon III was a bad patient. He was hypersensitive to pain, as his doctors and his dentist all knew,[46] though he bore pain with patience and real stoicism unless it was spontaneous and unexpected. The cutaneous neuralgia, for example, could drive him to extreme impatience. He was also inclined to hemorrhages and remembered several bad experiences after having had teeth extracted, once as a child and once in America, where he came briefly in 1837 after the Strasbourg fiasco. At that time an American surgeon told him that he did not know how to stop the flow of blood and that he would probably die. The dentist present then intervened and cauterized the wound. This episode left Napoleon with a durable faith in American dentists, though he thought the French variety were all charlatans.

[44] Gaspard, Baron Gourgaud, *Sainte-Hélène: Journal inédit de 1815 à 1818*, Paris: E. Flammarion, n.d., I, 309.

[45] "The Timidity of Surgeons Fifty Years Ago," *Journal of the American Medical Association*, LXXXIII (October 18, 1924), 1256.

[46] Dr. Thomas W. Evans, *op. cit.*, p. 14.

Because the emperor thought that there must be an immediate cure or remedy for every ill, he was not only quick to reproach his physicians when they could not produce instant results, but vulnerable to the promises of quacks who would tend to belittle the skills of conventional medicine—and vulnerable to the advice of his ignorant and arrogant chief valet de chambre, Léon Cuxac, who evidently counseled the emperor to ignore the prescriptions of his physicians and had in their place a ready supply of ancestral remedies.[47] The physicians could not obtain support through the Empress Eugénie, for she had as little faith in medicine and doctors as did the emperor. In any case, Dr. Conneau would probably not have confided in her, as he had a marked distaste for her;[48] we can only guess that his dislike stemmed from his knowledge of the unhappy marriage, for he was always discreet. As Dr. Barthez said, it was a very difficult environment in which to practice medicine effectively.

[47] Dr. Ernest Barthez de Marmorières, *The Empress Eugénie and Her Circle*, London: T. Fisher Unwin, 1912, pp. 30-39, 69, 221-224.

[48] Dr. Ernest Barthez de Marmorières, *La Famille impériale à Saint-Cloud et à Biarritz*, Paris: Calmann-Lévy, 1913, pp. 20-21, 119.

He got the hemorrhoids at Ham, justifying his aversion to the Orléans princes.

Prosper Mérimée

4 *Politics and Disease*

The mysteries of Napoleon III's mind and character were necessarily of interest to foreign governments in their concern to anticipate or interpret French policies, and because the emperor gave signs of physical distress from the earliest years of his reign the ambassadors' reports and the memoirs of that era were full of speculation as to its cause. Perhaps inevitably, ambassadors heard too much court gossip, and some of them, whether abhorring his political principles or contemptuous of his lineage, were only too ready to believe the worst. Most of the hostile memoirs and biographies, even if based upon private papers dating from the Second Empire, were compiled after the emperor's death. Earlier symptoms of his illnesses were made to square with the presumed cause of his death, allowing readers to overestimate how much Napoleon's contemporaries really knew about his medical details.

A related species of misinformation has been preserved by those memorialists who saw the emperor as obsessed by sex to the point that he was addicted to a life of pleasure. Thus, as Baron Beyens, the Belgian minister to France, saw it, the emperor early broke down and could not fulfill the demands of government. By 1859 he was presumably an old man in whom indecision and temporizing had replaced his earlier taste for spontaneous decisions and actions. Beyens inferred that the second half of the reign suffered from the "excesses" of the earlier years.[1] It did not occur to Baron Beyens, or to his generation for that matter, to suspect that the emperor's sexual difficulties stemmed from just the opposite of "excesses," and no doubt they would have found the notion offensive.

When Louis-Napoleon became president in 1848, the British ambassador in Paris was the Marquess of Normanby, a man known for his hostility to the new president. Normanby was even better known in Paris for his superficial knowledge of the French language, which was the cause of much merriment. The British foreign office found less amusement in his reports, which were described as tedious, lengthy, and usually full of irrelevant matters, though it seems extravagant to have expected

[1] Baron N.-E.-L.-J.-M.-A. Beyens, *Le Second Empire vu par un diplomate belge*, Paris: Plon-Nourrit, 1924-1926, I, 87-88.

better from a man who had published in 1828 a novel entitled *Yes and No.* In late January of 1852, Lord Granville could tolerate it no longer and asked for Normanby's resignation. The French post was first offered to Lord Canning, then to Lord Clanricarde, who both refused, and finally to Earl Cowley, then British minister to the Germanic Confederation at Frankfurt.[2] He would remain in Paris until 1867.

The British were fortunate in this third choice. One of Napoleon III's most perceptive biographers has correctly noted that Lord Cowley proved to have a far greater understanding of and sympathy for Napoleon than might have been expected of a nephew of the Duke of Wellington. What is more to the point, Cowley's reports home over a period of fifteen years were a marked contrast to the "painfully inadequate efforts" of the Austrian ambassadors to get to the bottom of Napoleon's character and intentions.[3] Baron Joseph von Hübner served Austria in Paris from 1851 to 1859, Prince Richard von Metternich-Winneburg from 1859 to 1871; their inadequacies were no small matter for the future of the Austrian empire, considering vital Austrian interests in Italy and Germany.

Napoleon's old friend, the Earl of Malmesbury, was invited to dinner at the Tuileries on March 20, 1853, about three weeks after the imperial marriage. Malmesbury had recently given up the foreign ministry and was at his ease as a private individual. The new empress cornered him to ask a great many questions about her husband,

[2] Lord Edmond Fitzmaurice, *Life of Earl Granville, 1815-1891*, London: Longmans, Green, 1905, I, 54-56.

[3] T.A.B. Corley, *Democratic Despot, a Life of Napoleon III*, London: Barrie & Rockliff, 1961, p. 124.

especially about his former health, and she wondered whether he was subject to headaches. She complained of the overheated rooms in the Tuileries, saying that they could not be cooled.[4] The emperor's own rooms in the palace were evidently deliberately overheated, probably in an attempt to soothe his rheumatism and neuralgia, and he enjoyed the warmth of a bed, often taking to bed during the daytime when he wanted to ponder a problem at length.[5] Contrary to what Baron Beyens would have us believe, the emperor's penchant for deliberation was already a habit by the time of his accession and not a quality that developed thereafter.

The months of the Crimean War were worrisome for him—and with good reason, considering the fumbling nature of Allied operations—and coincided with disappointment in his marriage. He soon began to reveal in public those symptoms of distress that we have already encountered in Dr. Ferguson's case-report (1856). On New Year's Day, 1855, when receiving the diplomatic corps for the customary greetings, he was suffering from either neuralgia or a mild attack of gout and was using a cane.[6] Ernest II of Saxe-Coburg had discussions with Napoleon in September of 1855, the very month that Sevastopol had at long last fallen to the Allies. The Russians at that point had shown no signs of a readiness to

[4] Malmesbury, *Memoirs of an Ex-Minister*, London: Longmans, Green, 1884-1885, I, 393.

[5] Augustin Filon, *Recollections of the Empress Eugénie*, London & New York: Cassell, 1920, p. 63.

[6] Count Alexander von Hübner, ed., *Neuf ans de souvenirs d'un ambassadeur d'Autriche à Paris, 1851-1859* (Joseph von Hübner), Paris: Plon, 1904, I, 304.

abandon the war, and no one yet knew how or when it could be ended. The signs of suffering on Napoleon's face were so alarming that Ernest was convinced that the emperor could not live much longer: "He was frequently tormented by such pains that he had to pause in his speech. When he was sitting, he was sometimes unable to rise without assistance. It was a very sad sight to see this man, who knew himself just arrived at the summit of his position, and secured in the possession of his power, in a state of the plainest physical decay."[7] Obviously the case of the forty-seven-year-old emperor was not as desperate as Ernest painted it. But Ernest was a sovereign duke in the German world; his brother was prince consort in England; his Saxe-Coburg relatives were the royal family of Belgium; so that his view of Napoleon, whatever its accuracy, helped to form the European estimate of the emperor's condition. It was not long before it was whispered that the emperor was suffering from a spinal disease, and some said that he was mad.[8]

In May of 1856, Dr. Robert Ferguson prescribed a diet, rest, and the use of what he called a "thermal spring." The empress told Lord Cowley that the emperor was following Ferguson's advice scrupulously, and, indeed, on July 2 he arrived at Plombières-les-Bains in Vosges to begin a three-week cure. In fact, he did not leave until August 8, presumably because the vacation agreed with him.[9] The mineral springs at Plombières featured a vari-

[7] Ernest II, *Memoirs*, London: Remington, 1888-1890, III, 193.

[8] Sir Victor Wellesley and Robert Sencourt, eds., *Conversations with Napoleon III*, London: E. Benn, 1934, p. 115.

[9] Jean-Dominique Haumonté, *Plombières ancien et moderne*, Paris: Champion, 1905, pp. 260-261.

ety of elements and temperatures. The first group of springs were warm arsenated sodium waters, varying in temperatures from twenty-seven to seventy-four degrees centigrade. These waters were used in baths, steamrooms, and showers by people suffering from gout or rheumatism, or by those seeking to sedate the nervous system. A second group of springs were soapy, laxative waters that were drunk cold and that contained bicarbonate of soda and calcium sulfate. Finally, there were waters containing a soluble iron oxide that had a distinctly metallic flavor. The physicians of that day prescribed different treatments depending upon whether the patient needed sedation or stimulation.[10] We do not know precisely what regimen was prescribed for Napoleon, but the chances are that he would have sampled everything available.

The emperor returned to Plombières in 1857 and remained from June 26 until August 1. However therapeutic, the waters could not provide a solution for his troubled love-life, and that autumn, at Compiègne with the Countess of Castiglione among the guests, Lord Cowley found him with a bad cold and in poor spirits.[11] His notorious affair was not bringing the solace he sought. In 1858, he returned to Plombières between June 30 and July 27, receiving Cavour there for two famous days of plotting against Austria on July 20-21. The Italian campaign followed in 1859, the emperor assuming supreme command.

[10] Dr. Constantin James, *Guide pratique aux eaux minérales de la France et de l'étranger*, Paris: Bloud et Barral, 1896, pp. 193-197; and Haumonté, *op. cit.*, pp. 66-69.

[11] F. A. Wellesley, ed., *The Paris Embassy during the Second Empire*, London: Butterworth, 1928, p. 136.

We know already Napoleon's deficiencies in military command, but it is unfair to add to them, as Baron Beyens did, by saying that the emperor was physically unfit for the campaign because of the dissipations that had aged him. Beyens found his proof in the fact that the emperor, though only fifty years of age, returned to Plombières for rest after a campaign that lasted little more than two months.[12] The fatigue was real, and there was good cause for it. Despite having left the empress as regent in Paris, Napoleon was still emperor as well as generalissimo, and he soon discovered that the new swift forms of communication, the telegraph and the railroad, brought him unexpected quantities of information and that he had not left political decisions behind when going to the front. Given his natural tendency to deliberate at length, the burden he consequently faced was extremely heavy, and he labored in the sure knowledge that military defeat would cost him the throne as well as the war. Early in the campaign his chief aide-de-camp recognized that the emperor would get no rest and predicted that the twin roles could not long be sustained by any man under the conditions of modern war.[13]

Much of the commander in chief's work did devolve upon others, as we know, but the emperor never escaped the responsibility for major decisions. At the battle of Magenta on June 4 he was overcautious during the early hours, but at the critical moment he gave the orders that brought MacMahon the encouragement and support he needed for victory. On June 24 the emperor's timely and skillful commitment of the imperial guard enabled

[12] Beyens, *op. cit.*, I, 87.

[13] General Comte Félix Fleury, *Souvenirs*, Paris: E. Plon, II, 13.

Forey's division to assault successfully a steep hill held by Austrian gunners and opened the way for the storming of the village of Solferino.[14] When the emperor got news of Prussian mobilization and possible intervention, he had to calculate the risk of following the Austrians as they retired into their fortified Quadrilateral. "I do not know what goes on in the emperor's mind," General Fleury wrote to his wife on July 4. "Evidently he is quite uncertain." Two days later he accompanied the emperor as he rode on a lengthy reconnaissance on the heights of Somma Campagna, studying the terrain against the possibility of continued fighting. The summer heat had become fearful, and Napoleon appeared to be extremely preoccupied, saddened by the high cost of the victories and aware of the difficulties ahead. When they returned to camp, he had decided to try for an armistice, and he sent Fleury to Verona with a letter for the Austrian emperor. Fleury, who knew that the sight of the dead and wounded had been very painful for Napoleon, did not believe that this personal horror affected the emperor's decision to cut the war short of complete victory. The reasons were military and political.[15] He had his armistice on July 11 and was able to take his rest at Plombières beginning August 9.

We can see in retrospect that the victory in Italy brought Napoleon to the pinnacle of his power and success, giving him options not before open to him. Yet his personal life was unhappy, and his very successes abroad were costing him old friends and allies. The British were suspicious that he was on the verge of becoming another

[14] *Ibid.*, II, 42-76.

[15] *Ibid.*, II, 107-113.

Napoleon I; the Belgians had never ceased to expect a French attempt at annexation; the Italians were angry that he had not done more for them in 1859; and many Germans, including his old friend Ernest II of Saxe-Coburg, feared that he might now take the lead in the German national movement after his success in Italy. As for his dynasty, by 1860 he had to face the fact that he was in his fifty-second year and his heir was only four. The history of regencies was hardly reassuring at best, and the well-known unpopularity of his empress meant that a regency in her favor could never be more than a temporary expedient. Many who saw him in 1860 were struck by his evident depression. During a Sunday lunch in Baden, where Napoleon met a number of German sovereigns that year, he seemed dispirited, and when a loud thunderstorm suddenly broke out he was evidently startled and made uncomfortable by it, repeatedly saying that he had never experienced anything so dreadful. By evening his spirits seemed to revive.[16]

It seems no mere coincidence, therefore, that the year 1860 was the transitional year for the Second Empire, the year in which he began to reconstitute his regime despite the objections of many in his entourage. Sometimes a reform, like the Cobden-Chevalier trade treaty of January 23, 1860, was desirable because it reassured the British of Napoleon's friendly intentions, quite apart from the importance of the treaty for French economic development. Sometimes a reform, like that outlined in the speech from the throne on November 24, 1860, promising the revival of legislative participation in government, was aimed at reconciling parliamentarians to the regime. But what

[16] Ernest II, *op. cit.*, IV, 36.

those reforms had in common with the remainder that would follow in the next decade was the spirit of liberalism, congenial both to the "ideas of '89" that the emperor believed he represented and to the practical problem of assuring the succession of his son.

It must be noted in passing, too, that the promise of greater liberties to come made by the emperor that November came only a few weeks after the terrible scenes he had experienced with Eugénie following the death of Paca. If he ever had reason to doubt her loyalty or competence, he had it that autumn. In the coming decade, both husband and wife would be devoted to the future of their son, the one by seeking to reduce executive authority, the other by struggling to retain it unimpaired. The marital estrangement, which was the foundation of the political estrangement, deepened with the passing years; only after the disaster of 1870 did the empress regain her affection and regard for her husband, seeing in him perhaps for the first time the strength and the goodness that had always been there.

The liberalization of the empire was also congenial to the emperor's scholarly disposition, and we see him return after 1860 to the studies interrupted by his escape from the University of Ham.[17] His research on the life of Julius Caesar,[18] an essay in defense of the great-man theory of history, amounted to a further elaboration of the Napoleonic tradition: "My goal is to prove that when

[17] Corley, *op. cit.*, p. 237.

[18] See Melvin Kranzberg, "An Emperor Writes History," in H. Stuart Hughes, *Teachers of History: Essays in Honor of L. B. Packard*, Ithaca, New York: Cornell University Press, 1954, pp. 79-104.

Providence creates men such as Caesar, Charlemagne, and Napoleon, it is to trace out the path which the peoples must follow, to mark a new era with the impact of their genius, and to fulfill several centuries' work in a few years. . . . Every day since 1815, this prophecy by the captive of St. Helena has been verified: 'How many struggles, how much blood, how many years will still be required until the good which I desire for humanity can be realized!' "[19] This retreat to a more sedentary life naturally spurred speculation about the emperor's ill-health, and he himself worried about the significance of his pains, though Conneau assured him that they derived from rheumatism, hemorrhoids, and neuralgia and were not serious.[20] "I feel better," Napoleon wrote to the empress in May of 1861, "but I confess that these deep pains in my legs disturb me, for I believe that they are the symptom of an illness which could be cured only if the doctors knew how to find the cause of it."[21]

Doctors Conneau and Andral did, however, advise the emperor to try the waters at Vichy that year, as they were somewhat more mineralized than those of Plombières—more alkaline, in fact. He went to Vichy for nearly a month, from July 4 to July 31, and then back to Plombières later in August.[22] But it is not true, though it is repeatedly written, that Dr. Félix Guyon probed the

[19] From the Preface to *Histoire de Jules César*, Paris: Imprimerie Impériale, 1865, I, vi-vii.

[20] Adrien Dansette, "La Maladie de Napoléon III," *la Revue de Paris*, LXX (September 1963), 37.

[21] Fernand Giraudeau, *Napoléon III intime*, Paris: P. Ollendorff, 1895, p. 406.

[22] Dr. Augustin Cabanès, *Les Morts mystérieuses de l'histoire*, Paris: Michel, 1923-1927, II, 408-409.

emperor for a urethral stricture in 1861; the point needs clarification because erroneous inferences were naturally drawn from such a significant operation. We can only surmise at this late date that the error derived in part from the fact that a Dr. *Guillon* would probe His Majesty in 1866, of which more later, and from the fact that Dr. Guyon aspired to treat the emperor in 1870.

For the record, Dr. Guyon (1831-1920) was a student of Dr. Velpeau, one of the emperor's consultants, and started his career in 1860 in what we would call gynecology, then hardly a field. He then moved into urology because it interested him, the opportunity coming upon the death of the famous specialist, Dr. Jean Civiale, who had invented the technique of crushing bladder stones (lithotrity) in 1823. Though without any particular preparation for such a practice, Guyon obtained Civiale's position at the Necker Hospital in 1867 on the recommendation of Velpeau, and became well known for urinary diagnosis and treatment. In 1870, when it was known in court circles that the emperor had urinary difficulties, Joachim Piétri (the second Piétri to be prefect of police) tried to arrange a consultation for the emperor with Guyon. Piétri had great confidence in Guyon, who had delivered Piétri's wife, but the consultation never took place.[23] Nor, in sum, had there been one in 1861.

In 1862, when Napoleon was very much resting on his laurels, devoting his mind to Roman history and hoping that the Académie française would crown his efforts with

[23] Dr. Jean-Louis Faure, *En marge de la chirurgie*, Paris: Les Arts et le Livre, 1927, I, 115-120.

an invitation to membership,[24] rumors persisted that he was planning a new war against Austria to obtain Venetia and that he planned to fight Prussia, if necessary, to gain the Rhine as a frontier. The British government asked Lord Cowley to appraise the rumors, and his response on January 10, 1862, was a fair measure of his excellent insight. However much the French might like to expand to the natural frontiers, he thought that the rumors were nonsense. He had never heard either the emperor or any of his ministers suggest a war to obtain the natural frontiers; rather, he said that they thought that any alteration of the 1815 settlement should be done through negotiations. Cowley knew, of course, that the emperor hoped that the map of Europe would be "remade" to make subject nationalities free and self-governing, in the interest of international peace. But the remaking of the map should be done peacefully and should include compensations to the powers who lost subject peoples. Cowley clearly thought that the portrait of Napoleon III as warlike was ridiculous, reminding his government of its difficulty in 1853 of persuading Napoleon to send a few thousand men to the Black Sea area, and of his lengthy hesitations after 1856 about supporting Sardinia-Piedmont, hesitations ended only by the foolhardiness of Austria in provoking the crisis of 1859. If Napoleon were guided by some masterplan designed to subject all of Europe, would such hesitations have appeared at all? Finally, Cowley noted the emperor's ill-health, his avowed horror of war as he

[24] Hortense Cornu to Nassau William Senior, "Louis-Napoleon Painted by a Contemporary," *Cornhill Magazine*, XXVII (Jan.-June 1873), 613-614.

had seen it, and his desire to pass on the empire to his son. Everything pointed to a policy of peace and to friendship with Britain.[25]

These observations were similar in spirit to those made by Madame Cornu to Nassau William Senior on April 7, 1862, which led to her reconciliation to Napoleon. She was received at the Tuileries on March 6, 1863, and began to see Napoleon regularly after that, sharing his concern for subject nationalities and for the destitute. As Ernest Renan said of her at the time of her death in 1875 (and reflecting his postwar bitterness), she had "all the noble errors of the time of her youth; she loved Italy, she loved Poland, she hated the strong and had predilection for the weak."[26] In a sense, Hortense Cornu resumed the role she had played at Ham, that of confidante and research assistant. In 1870 Napoleon would have her working on a plan to experiment with profit-sharing for workers in the mining industry.[27]

In 1863 Hortense Cornu met the empress for the first time, finding her charming but rather noticeably lacking information about political and social affairs.[28] Yet since 1860 Her Majesty had been increasingly speaking out on public issues, revealing a high sense of duty—which is not to say that the emperor allowed her to make public policy as a compensation for the "conjugal affronts" she had en-

[25] F. A. Wellesley, *op. cit.*, pp. 234-239.

[26] Marcel Emerit, *Madame Cornu et Napoléon III*, Paris: Les Presses Modernes, 1937, pp. 12-13.

[27] H. N. Boon, *Rêve et realité dans l'oeuvre économique et sociale de Napoléon III*, The Hague: Martinus Nijhoff, 1936, pp. 157-162.

[28] Hortense Cornu, *op. cit.*, p. 611.

dured. Perhaps had the marriage been happier, he could have curbed her more; perhaps he assumed that sophisticated diplomats and politicians would see her pronouncements for what they were worth and not suppose that she spoke for them both. On February 22, 1863, Prince Metternich reported home a conversation he had just had with Eugénie during which she reviewed for him a plan for the remaking of the map of Europe. The astonished ambassador, lacking Cowley's finesse, too readily inferred that he was being fed the emperor's own plan despite the fact that the empress honestly said to Metternich that she "wished to anticipate the emperor and at once go much farther than he."[29]

The French intervention in Mexico did not have its origin in the empress's mind, though she took great interest in it. Moreover, the emperor, far earlier than the empress, realized that the intervention was accomplishing deeds not anticipated by the French nor in the French interest. Probably neither Napoleon nor his ministers had ever intended the destruction of the Mexican Republic, yet they found themselves obliged by the exigencies of events to support the foundation of a Hapsburg monarchy. At a dinner at the Tuileries in March of 1864, honoring Maximilian and Carlota on the verge of their departure for Mexico, Ernest II overheard the two empresses enthusiastically discussing the situation in Spanish, certain that the monarchy would succeed. Their blissful confidence was not in the least shared by the Emperor Napoleon,

[29] The famous letter can be found in an appendix in Nancy Nichols Barker, *Distaff Diplomacy: The Empress Eugénie and the Foreign Policy of the Second Empire*, Austin: University of Texas Press, 1968.

who said to Ernest: "A very bad business. I, in her place, would never have accepted."[30]

Meanwhile, Napoleon had been persisting with his cures at Vichy, staying from July 11 to August 9 in 1862, July 7 to August 5 in 1863, and from July 7 to August 7 in 1864. Evidently the waters were palliative but did not cure, and in the summer of 1865 he returned to Plombières. Widespread rumors of his illness made the rounds, especially after he had a fainting spell at Biarritz in October of 1863, and another in August of 1864 after a visit to Marguerite Bellanger. The natural assumption was sexual overindulgence for a man of his age and responsibility, and, as we know, the empress intervened to put an end to the liaison.[31]

The signing of the Convention of September 15, 1864, by France and Italy only increased the empress's antagonism to the emperor. She seems periodically to have considered a separation,[32] always thinking better of it and preferring to try to get the emperor to abdicate in favor of a regency. The September Convention provided for the French withdrawal from Rome in two years in exchange for an Italian promise to protect papal integrity from revolution. Loyal Catholics like the empress had little faith in Italian promises when it came to Rome and regarded the Convention as a shameful abandonment of the Papacy. For Napoleon, however, the Convention was an important step in the liberalization of the Second

[30] Ernest II, *op. cit.*, IV, 175-176.

[31] Dansette, *op. cit.*, p. 38.

[32] E. A. Vizetelly, *Court Life of the Second French Empire*, New York: Charles Scribner's Sons, 1907, p. 205.

Empire, as the greatest ambiguity in his government had been in its religious policy. Officially and constitutionally anticlerical, the empire had protected clerical interests, and the French presence in Rome was the most notable symbol of that protection. What Napoleon did in 1864 more than forecast an end to the ambiguity: He gave clear indication, to those who wished to see it, that the empress did not dictate his policies. Perhaps the Austrians in particular did not get his message, because at the time they were preoccupied with suspicions that the September Convention contained secret clauses directed against them. In other words, they suspected an arrangement à la Plombières for the liberation of Venetia, something that in fact did not exist. Visiting Paris in October the former Austrian ambassador, Baron Joseph von Hübner, tried to assure his government that Napoleon was in too poor health to be thinking about starting a war, but the Austrians remained in uneasy mind about him.[33]

Napoleon's condition had been deteriorating since 1863. No longer was it simply a matter of arthritis, neuralgia, or hemorrhoids; now it was urinary difficulties. The medical record for 1863 and 1864 is unfortunately obscure, not simply because of the discretion of the imperial physicians, but because of the gossip which was later recorded as factual. Those who believed that the emperor had had more than ample opportunity to contract a venereal disease reached that welcome conclusion. One writer, seventy-eight years after the supposed event, dared to indict by innuendo the attractive ladies of Milan as the source

[33] John W. Bush, *Venetia Redeemed, Franco-Italian Relations, 1864-1866*, Syracuse: Syracuse University Press, 1967, p. 17.

of the imperial infection after the battle of Magenta.[34] No evidence of venereal disease was ever found,[35] and it is time to render justice to those ladies condemned wholesale.

What seems likely in view of the fragmentary evidence is that the emperor had begun to experience pain and difficulty in urinating, and that the cause was either gravel or the development of a stone in the bladder. As an arthritic who had already shown symptoms of gout, Napoleon was certainly liable to the development of calculi. Dr. Conneau, evidently suspecting a stricture of the urethra, occasionally used a catheter to try to enlarge the urethra, an unpleasant operation and done by a man with little expertise. The treatment could give no real relief, given the nature of the malady, but strengthened the imperial resolve to resist such attentions.[36]

The empress, in May of 1865, enjoyed a second brief period as regent when the emperor made a trip to Algeria. Ostensibly the trip was political, but it has logically been suggested that he sought an excuse for a vacation in a warm climate.[37] In his absence, the empress gave a series of dinners for small groups, especially including members of the Corps législatif; and during the evenings she talked matters of state with her guests. We can only surmise that she endeavored to enhance her political posi-

[34] G.C.N. Lecomte, *Napoléon III: sa maladie, son déclin*, Lyon: Les Laboratoires Ciba, 1937, pp. 18-19.

[35] Dr. Macdonald Critchley, "A Medical History of Napoleon III," *Second Empire Medley* (W. H. Holden, ed.), London: British Technical and General Press, 1952, p. 28.

[36] Dansette, *op. cit.*, p. 39.

[37] Vizetelly, *op. cit.*, pp. 336-337.

tion and reputation, anticipating a possible abdication by the emperor and aware that his cousin, Prince Napoleon, might well conspire to deprive her of the regency for her son.[38]

Napoleon made his regular visit to Vichy that July and then went to Châlons for the annual military maneuvers in August. On or about the fifteenth, the emperor had a particularly difficult night, and in the morning he summoned Baron Larrey for assistance. (The incident was not recorded at the time; hence the imprecision of the date.) Why, Larrey wanted to know, had the emperor not called him during the night? Because the emperor knew that Larrey had much to do, and besides he did not want "to arouse alarm."[39] Larrey then questioned the emperor about the symptoms and came to the conclusion that he was suffering from a bladder stone, but he made no examination of the patient. Instead, he explained as circumspectly as possible that His Majesty required immediate care and lengthy rest. He told the emperor that lithotrity was the only satisfactory way to deal with a stone and urged him to return to Paris immediately so that his regular physicians might conduct the necessary exploration to verify the existence of a stone. Baron Larrey also knew that the case was complicated by rheumatism and turgescent hemorrhoids, but he believed that the symptoms of a stone were undeniable.

The emperor firmly refused to return to Paris and told

[38] Marcel Blanchard, ed., "Journal de Michel Chevalier (1865-1869)," *Revue des deux mondes*, series 8, XII (November 1, 1932), 176-177.

[39] Emile Ollivier, "L'entrevue de Biarritz, 1865," *Revue des deux mondes*, period 5, IX (June 1902), 517-518.

Larrey that he could not follow the advice for "serious reasons," requesting that until further notice Larrey would say nothing to anyone about the diagnosis. Especially was the empress not to be informed.[40] Baron Larrey remained faithful to his pledge of silence and only in 1884, by which time the emperor had been dead for eleven years, did he reveal the diagnosis of 1865 in response to questions from Emile Ollivier. Subsequent speculation about the emperor's refusal to seek treatment centered on his sensitivity and his probable fear of further probing, yet we now know that he was to submit to such an operation eight years later. Some have thought that he lacked faith in such diagnoses after a dozen years of illness. On the other hand, at least since 1861 Napoleon had believed that he had an illness his physicians had not successfully diagnosed, so that it is reasonable to surmise that Larrey's ominous warning made sense to him. Furthermore, the emperor said not that he had serious doubts, but that he had *serious reasons* for avoiding a dangerous operation at that moment. He knew by then of the empress's desire to put him out to pasture and of Prince Napoleon's thirst for the throne; his unwillingness to risk lengthy incapacity or death until the prince imperial's succession should be assured is understandable.

Baron Larrey continued to accompany the emperor to the late-summer maneuvers at the Camp de Châlons after 1865,[41] but in Paris he found himself apparently banished from the Tuileries. He chafed in silence for nearly two years, then wrote a discreet letter to the grand chamber-

[40] Dr. L.-J.-B. Bérenger-Féraud, *Le Baron Hippolyte Larrey (1808-1895)*, Paris: Fayard frères, 1899, pp. 65-67.

[41] Val-de-Grâce, Carton 109.

lain to complain. His colleagues on the military Conseil de Santé had been repeatedly invited to concerts or dinners as guests of Their Majesties, and he could only conclude that he was being deliberately omitted.[42] In the aftermath, Larrey received clear evidence that he indeed enjoyed Napoleon's confidence, that the emperor no longer feared that the real seriousness of his condition would be whispered to the empress.

It would be useful to know just when the imperial couple first discussed the question of the emperor's abdication. On the basis of what the empress later said during an interview in 1903, we can infer that it took place between 1863 and 1866 and that Napoleon sidestepped the issue by allowing the empress to believe that he would not further liberalize the regime. At the same time he told her that liberalization must ultimately come but that it could be the work of the prince imperial after his accession. An unwritten agreement existed, therefore, that the imperial couple would abdicate in 1874 when the prince reached his eighteenth birthday. They would leave Paris to him, retiring to Pau for the winters and to Biarritz for the summers. Consequently she was surprised by the announcement of new liberal reforms on January 19, 1867, as a violation of their understanding.[43]

Such deceptions were not reserved for the empress alone. Napoleon's celebrated secretiveness intensified with the years and became more apparent as the regime faced a series of crises after 1863. What is more, he had never

[42] Bibliothèque Nationale, Nouvelles Acquisitions Françaises, 5889, Baron Larrey to the Duc de Bassano, March 24, 1867.

[43] Maurice Paléologue, *The Tragic Empress: Conversations of the Empress Eugénie, 1901-1919*, New York: Harper, 1928, p. 78.

been served by first-rate statesmen, and when death carried off the best he had (Billault on October 13, 1863, and Morny on March 10, 1865), he was all the more alone when crises came. Small wonder that he sought to escape from his burdens, decisions, and suffering, losing himself in study or reverie, seeing his ultimate salvation in a more liberal regime that would attract the service of able men. By 1866 the palace was rife with rumors of the total failure of his health, and his appearance was far from reassuring. He had grown stouter and seemed to be somewhat puffy, he was careworn and walked with evident pain.[44]

In such a condition he faced the shocking national dilemma that grew out of the Seven Weeks' War in the summer of 1866. When it came to the rivalry between Austria and Prussia in the Germanic world, the "Napoleonic idea" had always favored Prussia as a nation-state rather than cosmopolitan Austria. Parisian intellectual opinion shared that preference, not because it was a "Napoleonic idea," to be sure, but because Prussia presumably represented modern Germany, and Austria Catholic Germany. Outside Paris there was widespread indifference to German politics, as well as a general desire for peace that suggested a policy of French neutrality. Even though as early as 1854 Napoleon had remarked that the Germanic Confederation was as anachronistic as the Austrian presence in Italy and that he expected that Prussia eventually would be enlarged into Germany,[45] he had made no military commitment to Prussia as he did

[44] Anna L. Bicknell, *Life in the Tuileries Under the Second Empire*, London: T. Fisher Unwin, 1895, p. 200.

[45] Ernest II, *op. cit.*, III, 67.

to Sardinia-Piedmont in 1858. His policy was neutrality, all the Prussians wanted from him, and it was popular in the country.[46]

The Austrians wrongly suspected that the September Convention of 1864 masked an aggressive alliance between France and Italy for the recovery of Venetia, a mistake which left the Austrians in an uncomfortable position when facing the rising challenge from Prussia. For some months before 1866 French diplomacy endeavored in vain to obtain Venetia for Italy without a war by urging Austria to annex the Danubian principalities in exchange for Venetia, Turkey to be compensated financially by Italy upon receipt of Venetia. The upshot was a temporary alliance between Prussia and Italy, with Austria to be the victim. When war came in June of 1866, the Austrians hastily purchased French neutrality by ceding Venetia to France on June 12.

Had Austria won the war, as was anticipated by military opinion, or even had it been a stand-off, the French policies would have been deemed wise and fruitful. But on July 3 the Austrians failed to exploit a number of opportunities to win the battle of Sadowa, giving the Prussians an astounding victory.[47] On July 5, Napoleon summoned his ministers to Saint-Cloud to discuss what response France ought to make to this turn of events, for it had to be recognized that the overwhelming dimension of the Prussian success implied a drastic alteration in the balance of power in central Europe. Napoleon found that

[46] See André Armengaud, *L'Opinion publique en France et la crise nationale allemande en 1866*, Dijon: Bernigaud et Privat, 1962.

[47] John W. Bush, *op. cit., passim.*

members of his cabinet and his family were deeply divided over the issue. The pro-Austrian faction, which might also be called a Catholic faction, was led by the foreign minister, Edouard Drouyn de Lhuys, and the minister of war, Marshal Randon. They had the empress's support and wanted an immediate mobilization against Prussia to preserve Austria from a disastrous peace settlement. They estimated that by assembling no more than 50,000 men on the Rhine France would force Prussia to agree to make no territorial changes in Europe without French approval. In short, they were willing to risk war on behalf of Austria.[48]

Those who favored retaining the posture of neutrality were led by Eugène Rouher, the minister of state, and the Marquis de La Valette, minister of the interior, and found support from Prince Napoleon. By the end of the debate the emperor had joined this neutralist faction, and whatever he or historians may later have thought of the decision, it was sound at that moment, given both the immediate situation and the long-range view.[49] To risk war in the first place, when the army was unready and part of it deployed in Mexico, was unsound, as Napoleon knew better than Marshal Randon, especially considering that public opinion was profoundly antagonistic to another war. Second, to support Austria would have been to revert to a Catholic policy and to be inconsistent with the new liberal orientation, just as it would have been inconsistent with the Napoleonic principle of support for nationalities which wished to be self-governing. Finally,

[48] Paléologue, *op. cit.*, pp. 104-105.

[49] J. M. Thompson, *Louis Napoleon and the Second Empire*, Oxford: Basil Blackwell, 1954, p. 266.

Napoleon had obtained an unwritten promise in 1865 of territorial compensation along the Rhine from Bismarck as the reward for French neutrality, and Austria had already ceded Venetia to France. This meant that France would be a victor without a war, no matter which side won in central Europe; in case of the ultimate defeat of Austria, which now seemed probable, the Italo-Prussian allies would recognize French neutrality as having been benevolent. The emperor knew, too, despite Cowley's assurances to the contrary, that in Britain he was suspected of aggressive intentions. His persistent neutrality ought to revive British confidence in him and restore the alliance he valued more than any other.

In the days that followed the decision of July 5, the knowledge of what a cheap demonstration along the Rhine *might* have accomplished for French prestige evidently nagged the imperial mind, if not changing it; those who saw Napoleon in those days found him distressed. In general they attributed both his unrest and the decision to pursue neutrality to his obvious ill-health—a measure of how much Europeans were convinced of his bellicosity. The Count von Beust, a Saxon minister just then passing into the service of Austria and rightly thought to be on good personal terms with Napoleon, was asked on July 9 by the Austrian emperor to go to Paris to seek French intervention on behalf of Austria. He went at once and was immediately received by Napoleon. Failing in his mission, Beust recorded that he had had little hope of success once he had seen the emperor, explaining that Napoleon's intense pain had greatly impaired his physical and intellectual powers. Napoleon had repeatedly argued that France was not ready for war, and Beust kept insisting that no war would be necessary—merely a show of force on the Prussian frontier or on the North Sea. All Beust could get Napoleon to promise was to take Austria's part in the eventual peace negotiations out of consideration for having already received Venetia.[50]

Beust was not alone in creating the legend that the decision of July 5 and the subsequent adherence to it was a matter of poor health rather than a matter of lucid calculation. All Austrian and Prussian representatives who saw Napoleon in those weeks found him vague and seemingly undecided about his policy. In their concern for what he might do, their inability to penetrate his façade naturally caused anxiety; his evident ill-health was, for them, a logical explanation for his inaction. His unrest they attributed to indecision, not to the fact that he was living with an uncomfortable decision already made and was still subject to badgering on the matter by the empress. After a lengthy interview with Napoleon, Prince Reuss wrote to King William I on July 10 that the emperor was simply not himself. "I missed the calm and clarity which I associate with him."[51] The Prussian ambassador, Count von der Goltz, saw Napoleon the following day and reported home essentially the same thing: "The emperor seemed to have lost all sense of direction."[52]

An armistice was signed by Austria and Prussia on July 22, and four days later Prince Metternich, the regular Austrian ambassador, sent home two reports: the first of

[50] Friedrich Ferdinand, Count von Beust, *Memoirs*, London: Remington, 1887, I, 319-321.

[51] Wellesley and Sencourt, *op. cit.*, p. 289.

[52] Pierre de la Gorce, *Histoire du Second Empire*, Paris: Plon, 1894-1905, V, 38.

an interview with Napoleon, the second of an interview with the empress which he labeled "Very Secret." Since early in their embassy, the Metternichs had been on excellent terms with Eugénie, recognizing her partisanship and all too strongly inclined to see her as the chief architect of French policy. "I was witness yesterday," Metternich wrote in the first report, "to the uncertainties and to the extreme hesitations which characterize his state. He is very pale, very undone, and has the air of a man whose will power has had to give way to general exhaustion." Clearly Napoleon had been in great pain, and shortly after that audience he left for Vichy to obtain relief.

Metternich's second letter on July 25 reflected the empress's frustration and near hysteria, of which perhaps Metternich was the primary victim: "After my audience with the emperor, which left me with the most painful impression, I visited the empress. Her Majesty received me with tears in her eyes. She is very uneasy about the emperor's health and about *his physical and moral decay*, about which she gave the most convincing evidence. . . . The empress then told me that for a period of two years [the time of his liaison with Marguerite Bellanger], he had fallen into a complete prostration, no longer bothering himself with government, writing on *Julius Caesar* and giving it the little strength he had left. She told me that the meetings of the council of ministers, which she has been attending since that time, had given her obvious evidence of this exhaustion which no longer permitted the emperor to lead the council. He can no longer walk or sleep, and hardly eats, the empress added. . . . On Monday, the day before yesterday, the empress asked the emperor to abdicate and to confer the regency upon her.

. . . Never in the time that I have known the imperial couple have I seen the emperor so completely a cipher and the empress taking our interests to heart with such an extreme fury and zeal!"[53]

This appraisal must be set against Lord Cowley's letter on July 31. Cowley saw Napoleon daily in that critical period and knew perfectly well that he had been suffering bouts of fever and had gone off to Vichy on the twenty-eighth. "He suffers from rheumatism and neuralgic pains," Cowley wrote, "and like all of us is growing older. It is the fashion to say that his intellect is not what it was. I should rather say that it is in energy, not in intellect, that he is the worse for wear."[54] No doubt it would have been far better had the emperor been able to remain in Paris during the peace negotiations between Austria and Prussia,[55] especially since Bismarck seemed to be hedging on his promise to provide a Rhenish compensation for French neutrality.

The previous August, Baron Larrey had advised Napoleon against any further use of the Vichy waters, suspecting that they had either caused or contributed to the formation of the calculus he had diagnosed.[56] Yet Napoleon returned to Vichy on July 28, 1866, and, hardly arrived, he spent a dreadful night. Dr. Jean-Dominique Alquié

[53] Henry Salomon, *L'Ambassade de Richard de Metternich à Paris*, Paris: Firmin-Didot, 1931, pp. 140-141; and Comte E. C. Corti, "L'Empereur Napoléon III après Sadowa (1866)," *Revue des études napoléoniennes*, XIX (July-December 1922), 226-228.

[54] Wellesley and Sencourt, *op. cit.*, p. 303.

[55] Corley, *op. cit.*, pp. 286-287.

[56] Ollivier, *op. cit.*, p. 518.

(1793-1868) was summoned in the morning and was told that the emperor had not been able to urinate since the previous evening. Dr. Alquié, who had retired ten years before as the first director of the medical school at the Val-de-Grâce and had been given the title médecin inspecteur des eaux de Vichy as a sinecure,[57] hastily sought help from a surgeon named Guillon who was in Vichy for relief from gout. Dr. François-Gabriel Guillon (1793-1881) was as elderly as Dr. Alquié, but at least he was a specialist in urinary diseases; and it was known that he had been a consultant to King Louis-Philippe.[58]

On July 29 Guillon began the first of three treatments. He probed the emperor and then had him get into a warm bath, in which the emperor was able to urinate a little. After this session the emperor insisted on making a public appearance, probably in the hope of quieting gossip. A second probing took place on the morning of August 2, again followed by a warm bath. Because some fever and digestive upset followed these probings, Dr. Guillon was somewhat apprehensive; he asked that one of the imperial physicians be summoned from Paris. Dr. Rayer arrived on the third and, after examining the emperor, insisted that he leave Vichy. A third probing took place, however, in Rayer's presence just before the emperor's departure on August 7 for Saint-Cloud.

The tips of Guillon's probes had been rubber of tiny calibre mounted on olivewood handles, so that the soundings had been relatively painless and had cost no blood. In Saint-Cloud, Dr. Nélaton continued the treatments,

[57] Val-de-Grâce, Carton 203A, dossier 11.

[58] Val-de-Grâce, Carton 207[3], #754.

but used a silver catheter which caused pain and some bleeding.[59] The emperor's appearance left no doubt that he was miserable, and Goltz told Cowley that he genuinely wanted to obtain some territorial concession from Bismarck for the emperor, to ease his troubles.[60] The poor man then learned by telegraph that the Empress Carlota had landed at Saint-Nazaire on her way from Mexico to protest his decision to evacuate French troops from that unhappy situation.[61] That evacuation had been inevitable, especially after Napoleon had learned the true unpopularity of the Hapsburg monarchy, but the swift victory of Prussia produced the actual order to evacuate along with a recommendation that the Hapsburg couple abdicate and depart with the French.

Prosper Mérimée probably reflected court opinion when he described the emperor's ailment as hemorrhoids that were affecting his bladder. "As he is quite nervous and because he has had no exercise since the beginning of the war, he is on edge and irritated. A day of good weather will put him right. But instead of good weather, he has the empress of Mexico on his back. She arrived yesterday."[62] To Fanny Lagden, Mérimée wrote in English: "H.M. is always a little out of sorts nothing very important, but he works a great deal and I think he is

[59] Dr. Guillon (père), *le Courrier médical*, XIX (October 16, 1869), 327; and Dr. Cabanès, *op. cit.*, II, 413-415. Dr. Cabanès had the use of a letter written in 1890 by Guillon's son Alfred, which described the operations.

[60] Wellesley and Sencourt, *op. cit.*, Cowley to Lord Stanley, August 10 and 16, 1866, pp. 304-305.

[61] Paléologue, *op. cit.*, p. 113.

[62] Prosper Mérimée, *Correspondance générale*, Paris: Le Divan, 1941-1961, XIII, 172-173, Mérimée to Panizzi, Aug. 12, 1866.

much worried by M. de Bismark [*sic*] and by the empress of Mexico."[63] The following day he made a report to the Empress Eugénie's mother: "The emperor returned from Vichy in considerable pain. It appears that he has rheumatic pains and occasionally some fever. Nothing serious however. It all seems to me to have been provoked or developed by excessive work, perhaps by the bad temper that events in Germany have put him in. He is clearly better since his return. Yesterday he spent nearly the entire evening in the salon, and I saw return the facial expression he has when in good health and when he is happy. I do not think, however, that he will go to the Camp de Châlons, and this would, in my opinion, be the height of prudence on his part."[64] No doubt the emperor was worried about "M. de Bismark," for on August 23, when Austria and Prussia signed the Treaty of Prague, no compensation along the Rhine had yet been worked out for France.

Napoleon seemed, if anything, more secretive and mysterious to those who sought to plumb his mind than he had ever been before. One of the very diplomats who had ascribed French neutrality during the summer of 1866 to Napoleon's illness recognized that the emperor had evidently been restored to health after the trip to Vichy, yet continued to complain of the emperor's impromptitude of decision. He wrongly assumed that this illustrated a change in the emperor's nature, that formerly the emperor had been known for swift decisions. In fact, his description of Napoleon as a man who knew how to listen to others, who obviously listened carefully and weighed

[63] *Ibid.*, p. 179, Mérimée to Fanny Lagden, Aug. 15, 1866.

[64] *Ibid.*, p. 180, Mérimée to Mme. de Montijo, Aug. 16, 1866.

what was said to him yet avoided expressing himself categorically and promised nothing, was a description that would have been accurate long before 1866.[65] Perhaps therein lay much of the mystery of Napoleon III. All who talked to him thought they had his ear, that he was under their influence even when they could not get him to pronounce emphatically, and went away thinking of him as an amiable and cooperative man. In this particular case, the diplomat was a Hanoverian put in Paris specifically to promote war between France and Prussia, and not merely the emperor but also the wiser heads in the cabinet had been frustrating his goal.

And Napoleon was also continuing to escape Eugénie. She learned from Drouyn de Lhuys that he was being replaced as foreign minister by the Marquis de Moustier before she heard it from the emperor. Furious at the loss of the pro-Austrian minister, she pleaded with the emperor to abandon the policy of neutrality; failing absolutely, she again poured out her distress to the Austrian ambassador. In an astounding proposal, which among other things ought to have convinced Prince Metternich how little influence the empress had, she suggested to the Austrian that perhaps Bismarck could be induced to favor an Austro-Russo-Prussian entente, a possibility so grave for France as to force Napoleon to conclude an alliance with Austria. Her every effort, she told Metternich, would be for the future benefit of her son, further revealing the alienation of the imperial couple.[66]

[65] Oskar Meding, *De Sadowa à Sedan: Mémoires d'un ambassadeur secret aux Tuileries*, Paris: E. Dentu, 1885, p. 62, 130.

[66] Salomon, *op. cit.*, pp. 142-144, Metternich to Mensdorff, September 1, 1866.

In September the court moved to Biarritz for the annual season, and Napoleon, having paid Dr. Guillon 1000 francs for his three treatments in Vichy, now offered him 10,000 francs to come to Biarritz for a month. Reexamining Napoleon at Biarritz, Dr. Guillon noted the internal hemorrhoids and the irritated bladder but thought that the main problem was prostatitis, which he treated with poultices and enemas. Guillon was confident that the treatment had been successful, noting that the emperor was able to ride horseback at the Camp de Châlons that October. Guillon also observed sand in the imperial urine and thought there should be further exploration of that problem, but it was not done because the personal physicians believed it to be unnecessary.[67]

In any case, his health did seem to be returning, as Mérimée repeatedly charted in his letters, admitting that there were little crises of pain now and then, that the emperor seemed sadder and more pessimistic than formerly. But then why not? For even the most stoic of men would have been depressed by the avalanche of misfortunes he was beginning to bear—from Mexico, Prussia, and Italy. Even so, he was doing marvelously, Mérimée thought, and walking two leagues every day.[68] Certainly the foreign news was entirely bad, and it got worse in 1867.

Bismarck, in the first place, betrayed his promise to Napoleon, preventing any cession of Rhenish territory to France, suggesting the purchase of Luxembourg from the

[67] Dr. Guillon, *op. cit.*, p. 328; and Dr. Cabanès, *op. cit.*, II, 415.

[68] Mérimée, *op. cit.*, XIII, 217-250, Mérimée to Mme. de Montijo, October 3, 1866; to Princess Julie de Roccagiovine, Oct. 6, 1866; and to Mme. de Beaulaincourt, Oct. 15, 1866.

king of the Netherlands as an alternative compensation, and then scuttling that bargain when the king proved willing to sell. It was a shabby return for the benevolent neutrality of 1866 and enabled those who read history backwards to label that neutrality a catastrophic mistake. The real mistake was Bismarck's failure to understand that Napoleon had long since accepted the legitimacy of Prussian aggrandizement in Germany. Instead, he made Napoleon his dupe and fomented a sense of great outrage in France. In the background was the French evacuation of Mexico, the admission of another policy gone sour. The execution of the Emperor Maximilian on June 19, 1867, was the dreadful end for those who had assisted him to power. When the French imperial couple visited the Austrian imperial family at Salzburg two months later, it was thought that the French party seemed somewhat ill at ease over the Mexican tragedy, perhaps the understated observation of 1867. Napoleon was seen at Salzburg as considerably aged during the previous eighteen months, walking slowly and stiffly as if with some difficulty. But he also appeared to be in good health: tanned, stout, and upright.[69]

Also evident in 1867 was Italian ingratitude for Venetia. The Italians had been defeated on land and sea by the Austrians in 1866. Yet they came out on the winning side, thanks to the Prussian victory and French neutrality, and Napoleon handed them a province they had done little to gain. Italian pride was seriously wounded, and the French paid the price for Italian failure. The French evacuation of Rome under the terms of the September

[69] W. Beatty-Kingston, *Monarchs I Have Met*, London: Chapman & Hall, 1887, I, 146.

Convention of 1864 was followed by Garibaldi's attempt to seize the city for Italy in violation of that convention. Rather than risk the posture of a total sellout of the Pope, the French had to reoccupy the city, in the process wounding the great Italian hero at Mentana (November 3, 1867). More than French foreign policy suffered in this embarrassment, for the continued French presence in Rome compromised the liberalizing empire in the eyes of anticlerical liberals. This situation was a powerful factor in making the Liberal Empire, when it came in 1870, a Liberal *Catholic* Empire; not to speak of the painful fact that when France required an ally in 1870, the Italians were looking south.

In the meantime the emperor's health continued to improve during 1868. Having heard the continual rumors to the contrary, Baron Vitzthum wrote that he was astonished to find the emperor sparkle with animation. He "gave me the impression of a man aroused from a distressing nightmare. His mind generates the light and life returns to him with the dawn."[70] Six months later Metternich reported in the same vein: "I have never found the Emperor better, both in health and spirits, or more forthcoming, than he was during the short visit I have just paid him."[71] In July, the emperor went back to Plombières—no more trips to Vichy—for his rheumatism, Mérimée believed, and seemed still in good health upon his return to Fontainebleau in August. "He seems much better than I have seen him for a long time."[72] Only Lord

[70] Wellesley and Sencourt, *op. cit.*, p. 345, Vitzthum to Beust, Jan. 19, 1868.

[71] *Ibid.*, p. 348, Metternich to Beust, July 3, 1868.

[72] Mérimée, *op. cit.*, XIV, 209, Mérimée to Mme. de Montijo, Aug. 10, 1868.

Lyons, who had come to Paris following the retirement of the reliable Cowley in 1867, sent home repeated pessimistic reports on Napoleon's health in 1868, but even he admitted before the end of the year that the emperor seemed to be well and in good spirits.[73]

For the first half of 1869 the emperor's good fortune continued. His health seemed excellent, and he walked a great deal for exercise.[74] By mid-August, however, the old pains of 1866 began to trouble him, giving him sleepless nights.[75] His minister of war, Marshal Niel, had been bedridden since the first of the month with symptoms of a bladder stone. Dr. Nélaton was called in and decided to operate. He thought that the lithotrity had been successful, but Niel quickly developed a high fever, dying on August 13. It was a double blow for the emperor. To make his discomfiture worse, a brilliant young surgeon, formerly a student of Nélaton, publicly charged that Nélaton had bungled the operation, causing Niel's death. These charges by Dr. Jules-Emile Péan were of course denied—and also generally believed. That the emperor had not visited Niel's deathbed was taken in Paris as a sure sign that the emperor himself was again ill; this was confirmed when an audience granted to Marshal Prim on August 27 had to be postoned.[76]

[73] Lord Newton, Thomas Wodehouse Legh, *Life of Lord Lyons*, London: Longmans, Green, 1913, I, 197-206, Lyons to Clarendon, Dec. 15, 1868.

[74] Mérimée, *op. cit.*, XIV, 487-539, Mérimée to Mme. de Montijo, May 11, 1869, and to Princess Mathilde, July 9, 1869.

[75] Goncourt, *Journal*, Paris: Charpentier, 1891-1907, III, 313.

[76] Germain Bapst, *Le Maréchal Canrobert. Souvenirs d'un siècle*, Paris: Plon, 1903-1904, IV, 115-116.

The empress, meanwhile, had been for some time scheduled to make an official visit down the Rhone valley and to Corsica. Accompanied by Baron Larrey, she left Saint-Cloud on August 23,[77] suggesting that the emperor's new pains were not being taken very seriously. Dr. Ricord and Dr. Nélaton were both consulted, and for a time there was talk of calling in a specialist from Heidelberg, but nothing was done.[78] The physicians gave assurances that the difficulties were painful but not alarming, though they were unable to halt rumors to the contrary.[79] When Baron Larrey returned from Corsica, he found the pessimism at Saint-Cloud so thick that he asked to be excused from accompanying the empress on a second trip, this time to Suez for the opening of the canal. He feared that he might inadvertently communicate his alarm to the empress.[80]

Why had nothing been done? The physicians' tendency to procrastinate when faced with such a responsibility was no doubt sharpened by Nélaton's recent unpleasantness, and presumably the emperor's reluctance was unchanged. In all fairness, too, we must recognize that the risk was great, for the state of urinary medicine in the eighteen-sixties gave no cause for confidence. Lithotrity, the crushing of bladder stones, had been developed by the late Dr. Civiale in 1823 to replace the various methods

[77] Val-de-Grâce, Carton 109.

[78] Dr. Cabanès, *op. cit.*, II, 416.

[79] Mérimée, *op. cit.*, XIV, 603-605, Mérimée to Jenny Dacquin and to Panizzi, Sept. 7, 1869.

[80] Bibliothèque Nationale, Nouvelles Acquisitions Françaises, 5889, Larrey to Conneau, Sept. 21, 1869; and Bérenger-Féraud, *op. cit.*, p. 67.

of cutting for the stone that had been practiced since antiquity. The modern procedure, however, was limited by inadequate equipment, and even after the invention of the urethrotome in 1862 by Dr. Maisonneuve the great danger from infection remained. Nélaton, as we know, improved a catheter for urinary use in 1863 by constructing it of flexible rubber, but despite these advances there were surgeons who were suspicious of lithotrity and continued to recommend some form of lithotomy. Dr. Félix Guyon, who came to urology late in the eighteen-sixties, somewhat later became the first surgeon to adopt the modern antiseptic methods which revolutionized urinary surgery, but these were not the techniques of 1869. To postpone, therefore, was not simply a matter of cowardice; the operation had to be the last resort.[81]

As the physicians watched in September of 1869, the emperor began to improve. By the twelfth he was recovering his usual routine, and on the fourteenth he received the postponed Marshal Prim, who had a matter about the vacant Spanish throne to discuss. Prince Metternich thought that the emperor was notably pale and weak, with the appearance of a man who had been in bed for weeks, but found his language clear and precise.[82] The recovery was slow, he often dozed in his chair, and those around him were aware that he was an old man. Some members of the empress's circle encouraged her to assume a regency,[83] but by then the final steps to create the Lib-

[81] Dr. Faure, *op. cit.*, pp. 121-122.

[82] Wellesley and Sencourt, *op. cit.*, pp. 350-352, Metternich to Beust, Sept. 20, 1869.

[83] Commandant Schneider, *Le Second Empire à Saint-Cloud*, Paris: Victor-Havard, 1894, pp. 6-8.

eral Empire, a limited monarchy, were well under way. When the court moved to Compiègne in November, the American minister said that he had found Napoleon not merely in good health but in fine spirits.[84] And why not? He had survived to be on the verge of reconstituting his regime and thus, in his mind, of securing his son's succession.

[84] E. B. Washburne, *Recollections of a Minister to France, 1869-1877*, New York: Charles Scribner's Sons, 1889, I, 15-16.

It was plain that death would have nothing to do with him. The big drops of anguish had washed the rouge from those painted cheeks, the waxed mustache had lost its stiffness and drooped over the mouth, and in that ashen face, in those dim eyes, was the stupor of one in his last agony.

Emile Zola

5 *War and Death*

The coming of the Franco-Prussian War in July of 1870 has always been a troublesome historical problem, and both the origins and the outcome of the war have been linked traditionally to the health of Napoleon III. The year had begun propitiously. On January 2, a liberal regime had taken office dedicated to working out the format for a limited monarchy, and one of the conditions the liberals laid down in taking office was that the Prussian gains of 1866 be regarded as legitimate and not a cause for revenge despite the French failure to obtain the promised compensation. As a measure of its good faith, the new regime let it be known that it favored a reduction of European armament. Even though Berlin rejected such a prospect, the liberal regime did not take alarm. Its eye was on domestic and constitutional reform.

In one respect the emperor shared the optimism of the new government. "Nothing has been more interesting nor more extraordinary," wrote Ludovic Halévy on January 4, 1870, "than this perfect calm on the emperor's part during this parliamentary crisis. Here is a man who, six months ago, one can say had France in his hand. . . . He has calmly let it all go. Those around him [the conservative Bonapartists] are dismayed, the empress irritated. Around him the emperor sees only somber and anxious faces. 'What is the matter,' he says to everyone, 'never has it been so orderly during a revolution.' The word is apt and true."[1] When it came to Prussia and Bismarck, however, the emperor as the primary victim of Bismarck's deviousness in 1867 was less sanguine than his ministers. Against the uncertainties of the future, he sought an alliance the more needed, in his mind, since Marshal Niel and he had failed in 1868 to get the nation to accept significant military reforms. He would have preferred a British alliance, but except for Lord Clarendon, who suspected future trouble from a Prussianized Germany, British politicians regarded Napoleon as their most serious menace.[2] The Italians were in no mood to be pleasant,

[1] Ludovic Halévy, *Carnets*, Paris: Calmann-Lévy, 1935, II, 36-37.

[2] W. E. Mosse, *The European Powers and the German Question, 1848-1871*, Cambridge: Cambridge University Press, 1958, pp. 300-303.

and Russia was closely associated with Prussia in their common concern to keep the Poles subjugated. There remained only Austria. Accordingly, Napoleon sent one of his trusted military aides, General Joseph Lebrun, to Vienna to see what manner of acceptable alliance could be achieved.

As for the emperor's health, the recovery from the crisis of August, 1869, had been real enough when observed on a day-to-day basis. But time was taking its toll, spurred on by the frightful pain of his periodic illnesses and by the run of bad luck he had experienced in his governance. Those who saw him after a lapse of two or three years found him much altered in appearance and looking very much the sick man despite his recovery, much older than his sixty-two years.[3] Lord Lyons thought the emperor's new government had a good chance for survival, noting that even Eugénie had admitted to him that the murder of Victor Noir by Prince Pierre Bonaparte early in 1870 would have been far more threatening to the old regime than it had proved to be to the new.[4] But Lyons also predicted that should Prussia provoke more trouble she would be met more decisively by *any* ministry than she had been by the emperor in 1867. Only a few years before, statesmen had counted on Napoleon's bad health to prevent war. Now the fear was that the emperor's

[3] Third Earl of Malmesbury, James Howard Harris, *Memoirs of an Ex-Minister*, London: Longmans, Green, 1884-1885, II, 413-415.

[4] Lord Newton, Thomas Wodehouse Legh, *Life of Lord Lyons*, London: Longmans, Green, 1913, I, 244, Lyons to Clarendon, Jan. 18, 1870.

views and bad health could no longer be counted on to prevent war.[5]

The empress was, as Halévy put it, highly irritated by the constitutional changes, as they reflected the ultimate defeat of her political views. Even years later, when she had considerably mellowed, she still remembered Napoleon in the spring of 1870 as "practically counting for nothing": because of his illness, yes, but particularly because he had surrendered the right "to act arbitrarily" against his ministers.[6] Others at court, however, were more charitably disposed toward His Majesty at that moment, genuinely concerned about the urinary condition that they knew existed, and pressed the emperor to seek medical aid from beyond the imperial medical staff. Joachim Piétri, who had great personal loyalty to Napoleon, wanted the emperor to consult Dr. Félix Guyon, in whom Piétri had great confidence. Piétri held Dr. Guyon in readiness for a number of mornings in the hope that the emperor would consent to see him, but in vain.[7]

The Duchesse de Mouchy, née Anna Murat and a relative of Napoleon, had better luck. She had great confidence in Dr. Germain Sée (1818-1896), who had been treating members of the Murat family for a number of years. He had been a professor of therapeutics on the Paris faculty since 1866, and his growing reputation caused him to be elected to the Académie de médecine in July of 1869. Although he had wide interests in inter-

[5] *Ibid.*, I, 285, Lyons to Clarendon, May 6, 1870.

[6] Maurice Paléologue, *The Tragic Empress: Conversations of the Empress Eugénie, 1910-1919*, New York: Harper, 1928, p. 126.

[7] Dr. J.-L. Faure, *En marge de la chirurgie*, Paris: Les Arts et le Livre, 1927, I, 119; and Police dossier E a/22 7.

nal medicine, Dr. Sée was beginning to specialize in gout and rheumatism.[8] Thanks to Anna Murat, the emperor agreed to receive him at Saint-Cloud on June 19, 1870.[9] What Sée learned of the case from Anna Murat, and what he learned from the emperor in private conversation on the nineteenth, led him to diagnose initially the presence of a bladder stone, but he wanted a board of specialists convened to verify this suspicion.[10] What Napoleon had refused to do in 1865 at Baron Larrey's request he now agreed to permit at Dr. Sée's request, and a consultation was scheduled for eight o'clock on the morning of July 1. Larrey's earlier diagnosis was still a secret, and nothing emerged from the consultation of July 1 to permit us to believe that even Dr. Sée was aware of that earlier diagnosis.

We might immediately wonder why the emperor, at the request of a physician hardly known to him, permitted a consultation that might well lead to publicity about a bladder stone when he had earlier demanded secrecy. No precise evidence exists to explain the emperor's change of mind, but at least one explanation has been given, based largely on circumstantial evidence, that needs refuting. Lord Acton, evidently unaware that Dr. Sée had visited the emperor as early as June 19, rather ingeniously noted that the medical consultation of July 1 occurred several days after General Lebrun's return from his mis-

[8] Archives Nationales, F17 3685.

[9] Paul Guériot, *Napoléon III*, Paris: Payot, 1933-1934, II, 142.

[10] Dr. E.-G. Sée, "Un grain de sable dans la vessie d'un empereur," *le Mercure de France*, 292 (June 15, 1939), 595; and Edward Legge, *The Empress Eugénie 1870-1910*, London: Harper, 1910, pp. 79-80.

sion to Vienna; this fitted Acton's belief that Napoleon's intention was an *offensive* alliance against Prussia. Acton saw the physical examination, coming as it did when the emperor's suffering was not more intensive than usual, as part of the preparation for war. In other words, was he fit for command?[11]

The inadequacy of this explanation is twofold: Recent studies make it abundantly clear that Napoleon III sought to solve the German problem by negotiation, and that he was not planning war.[12] And, as we shall see, his physical fitness to command was irrelevant. He believed that he had no option but to command, in sickness or in health. Lord Acton knew, of course, that no Franco-Austrian alliance yet existed but assumed that it was well along in the making. What *really* had occurred, however, was popular sanction of the Liberal Empire through plebiscite that April. Even though many constitutional and procedural problems remained to be ironed out, Napoleon could for the first time have some confidence that he had at long last accomplished the security of his fourteen-year-old son's succession to the throne.

The consultation of July 1 took place at the residence of Dr. Conneau, but he was present merely as a witness to the proceedings. In addition to Dr. Sée, the participants

[11] Baron Acton, J. E. E. Dalberg-Acton, "The Causes of the Franco-Prussian War," *Historical Essays and Studies*, London: Macmillan, 1907, pp. 208-212.

[12] See William E. Echard, "Conference Diplomacy in the German Policy of Napoleon III, 1868-1869," *French Historical Studies*, IV (Spring 1966), 239-264; and Richard Millman, *British Foreign Policy and the Coming of the Franco-Prussian War*, New York: Oxford University Press, 1966.

were Doctors Corvisart, Nélaton, Ricord, and Fauvel, all members of the imperial household. What went on during the consultation is not entirely clear. Evidently Dr. Sée presented his findings to the group and recommended an exploratory sounding of the emperor as the preliminary step to a probable operation to crush the stone. In the ensuing discussion, he was able to convince only Dr. Ricord of the diagnosis. Corvisart thought that the symptoms revealed nothing more serious than a bladder catarrh, and Nélaton seemed to agree. Consequently, when it came to the proposal to sound the emperor, the committee stood two against three; Nélaton saying that he would probe an ordinary patient, but not this one.[13]

The report of the consultation was written by Dr. Sée. It has been said that this task fell to him because custom required the youngest physician present to write the report.[14] In fact Dr. Sée was not the youngest physician at the consultation—Dr. Corvisart was six years his junior—and the matter is not trivial, because Sée's signature was ultimately the only one fixed to the document. His report consisted of four diagnostic sections, followed by a brief recommendation for treatment:

> 1) Cutaneous or muscular hypersensitivity of anemic origin. [Anemia then meant a deficiency of blood characterized by paleness and fatigue rather than the more precise deficiency of red corpuscles as we understand it.] This hypersensitivity is manifested by surface pains on the skin of the thighs, pains which are aggravated by the slightest touch, but, conversely, can be reduced

[13] Dr. E.-G. Sée, *op. cit.*, pp. 596-597; and Legge, *op. cit.*, p. 81.

[14] Dr. Augustin Cabanès, *Les Morts mystérieuses de l'histoire*, Paris: Michel, 1923-1927, II, 418.

by pressure or revived by a variety of influences, especially by cold. There is great sensitivity in the muscles near the joints of the feet where they are attached to the limbs—whether spontaneous or induced; and this sensitivity, in the form of shooting pains, also occasionally appears when influenced by cold. This does not prove [the pains] to be rheumatic; everything that cold induces is not rheumatic. The patient has never had rheumatism in his joints, even though these pains date from his twentieth year; which is to say from a period when there were two serious causes of anemia. [Apparent reference to youthful hemorrhages.] Such neuromuscular hypersensitivities, in fact, are nearly always due to anemia.

2) Other than these pains, there remains hardly any evidence of the anemia that was much more evident earlier. It was due to an imprisonment of six years, which is to say, to an insufficient exercise in open air and to mental influences. One physical cause to be added to these diverse causes of anemia is a very considerable hemorrhoidal flux, a nearly constant factor especially for the past six years. Today, the anemia has nearly disappeared. There is no wind sound in either the tubes or the heart. The heart-beat and the noises in that organ are faint but perfectly regular. There is no trace of palpitations, and if there have been several fainting spells in the past, it only proves that the anemia still existed, but no heart disease.

3) Some gouty phenomena have been apparent here and there and in the joints of the feet—and recently; but no accompanying rheumatism and no other interior complications except for a lesion in the bladder. From

time to time there has been a swelling of the abdomen, sometimes from the sensitivity of the stomach and the intestines. But this is usual in those with hemorrhoids. Thus, we conclude in saying that these digestive troubles, just as the peripheral pains, are due to the hemorrhoids and to the resulting anemia. But it remains to interpret the lesion of the bladder.

4) The weakening of the urinary passages: In the past five years there have been four hematurias. Following the one in [1866] the urine remained muco-purulent for a year, then cleared up. Beginning in August of 1869, when there were sharp and deep pains in the urinary organs, the urine has contained a certain amount of pus, estimated at a minimum of one-fortieth to one-fourth or one-third of the total urine during the worst period. There has also been some dysuria; very marked slowness to urinate in the morning, and interruptions in the stream of the liquid at other times. Occasionally there have been such difficulties as to require a probe. That is what happened at Vichy [four] years ago and in the month of August, 1869. Since that time it should be noted that horseback riding and the jolting of carriages often arouses pain in the kidneys, in the lower stomach, or in the fundament. A malady characterized by these three phenomena: 1) repeated hematurias; 2) purulent urination for nearly three years with impairments more or less marked; 3) frequent dysuria characterized by spasm and inertia in the bladder; can be diagnosed only as a calculous pyelocystitis. If there had been only purulent urinations, one could believe this to be a simple catarrh. If we did not have to take into account what had happened before

the month of August, 1869, we might think this to be a perivesical abscess in the urethra. But the interior hemorrhaging, the persistence of the purulent urines for a year, the frequent return of the dysuria, and the increase in the pains through the jolting, necessarily leads us to think this to be a cystitis of a calculous origin and that this calculus is located and fixed in the bladder, possibly having originally been located in the kidneys. In addition, there has been on occasion an excess of uric acid and of urates in the urine.

That is why we shall consider the examination of the bladder with a catheter as necessary, an exploration; and we think that the present moment is opportune as there is not at present any painful phenomenon. In fact, if the dysuria, the purulence, or the pains reappeared or increased, we would have to fear provoking an acute inflammation by an exploration.

The report was signed by Dr. Sée alone and dated Paris, July 3, 1870.[15] The failure of the other members of the committee to sign the report was only the first of the mysteries regarding its fate. Not all members of the committee, to be sure, agreed with all aspects of the report, but neither did they submit a contrary view. When Dr. Sée had completed his report he gave it to Dr. Conneau, asking that Conneau obtain the others' signatures. Evidently Conneau did not ask the other consultants for their signatures, either because he thought it was unnec-

[15] Dr. Amédée LaTour published the case-report in *l'Union médicale*, XV (Jan. 9, 1873), 25-27. LaTour was a friend of Dr. Sée, who verified the authenticity of the document for the medical journal. See *Lancet*, I (January 1873), 105; and *Journal des connaissances médicales pratiques*, XL (January 1873), 7-9.

essary to have them or because he had reason to believe that Dr. Nélaton would refuse to sign. Dr. Ricord was later to say that Nélaton feared that if the diagnosis were accepted he would have to operate, and that after his failure with Marshal Niel he did not want such a responsibility. Ricord added that Nélaton had not actually refused to sign the document, merely that he had not asked to sign it. The remaining consultants followed his example.[16] This lack of unanimity and the evident equivocation put poor Dr. Conneau in a dilemma; to understand the full dimensions of the dilemma we must realize that what had been simply a medical question on July 1, the day of the consultation, had become political as well with the astonishing news of the Hohenzollern candidacy for the Spanish throne on July 2.

What Dr. Conneau did with his information has never been exactly known, nor can we know precisely what he thought of Dr. Sée's diagnosis. The document was found in his papers in the Tuileries after the fall of the Second Empire,[17] from which we may reasonably infer that whatever he communicated to the imperial couple he did verbally. Prince Napoleon was probably responsible for distorting the record, whether intentionally or otherwise. At a dinner in 1879, he stated that the original document was found in the emperor's papers after his death, following which Prince Napoleon had questioned Dr. Conneau

[16] Alfred Darimon, *Notes pour servir à l'histoire de la guerre de 1870*, Paris: Paul Ollendorff, 1888, pp. 31-32.

[17] "Consultation du Docteur G. Sée sur la santé de l'Empereur à la veille de la guerre," *Papiers et correspondance de la famille imperiale*, Paris: Imprimerie Nationale, 1870-1872, II, 59-61. This document is *not* found in most editions of the "Papiers sécrets."

about it. According to Prince Napoleon, all Conneau would say is that he had shown the report to the one who had the right to see it, and that person had responded: "*Le vin est tiré; it faut le boire.*"[18] Prince Napoleon inferred, and Lord Acton later concurred, that "the one who had the right to see it" had been the Empress Eugénie. Her response presumably reflected her desire to let nothing interfere with a showdown with Prussia over the Hohenzollern candidacy.[19] The implication is that she stubbornly pressed her husband toward war and the supreme command of the armies in the foreknowledge that it would lead to his physical collapse or death, her last grasp for the regency.

We may attribute this interpretation to Prince Napoleon's well-known hatred for the empress. Augustin Filon, in charge of the prince imperial's education from 1867 to 1875, and secretary to the empress during her brief regency in 1870, said that Dr. Sée's document had been sought in the emperor's papers after his death but *not* found. Its existence was known because of its publication in a number of journals in 1873, and therefore Prince Napoleon could have been able to question Dr. Conneau as he said he did. Filon thought that Prince Napoleon's interpretation of Conneau's response was completely wrong and believed that the empress knew nothing of Sée's diagnosis at that time.[20] Years later the empress would say that Dr. Conneau had mentioned nothing more serious than rheumatism and cystitis to her and

[18] Darimon, *op. cit.*, pp. 32-33.

[19] Lord Acton, *op. cit.*, p. 212.

[20] Augustin Filon, *Recollections of the Empress Eugénie*, London: Cassell, 1920, p. 259.

had given her no hint of anxiety when the emperor decided to assume the supreme command that month.[21] When Marshal Leboeuf asked her if the emperor's health would allow him to lead the army, she answered that he certainly would be able to in warm weather, but that the winter cold would bring back his pains. "In this season he is very well able to command."[22] And, finally, are we to believe that this devoted mother would have permitted the fourteen-year-old heir to the throne to have accompanied Napoleon on the campaign had she known of the ominous diagnosis of July 3? Whatever her failings in politics or as a wife, she was too high-minded to merit Prince Napoleon's vile implications.

Some have argued, on the contrary, that it stretches credibility to suppose that in the great national crisis between July 2 and July 19 (when war came) the imperial couple was ignorant of the Sée diagnosis. The proponents of this view hold that it makes no sense to suppose that Dr. Conneau would deliberately have misled the empress under those serious circumstances and that the imperial couple together were responsible for what amounted to a dynastic decision. That is, they would keep his ill-health a secret from the cabinet, and the emperor would abdicate as soon as a limited military victory had been achieved and a peace settlement signed. This would postpone a risky operation until the heir had succeeded to the throne.[23]

One of the two major flaws in that particular conjec-

[21] Paléologue, *op. cit.*, pp. 138-140.

[22] Adrien Dansette, "La Maladie de Napoléon III," *la Revue de Paris*, LXX (September 1963), 44.

[23] Dr. Gustave-Jules Witkowski, *Comment moururent les rois de France*, Paris: Bibliothèque des Curieux, 1920, p. 191.

ture is that Napoleon III, as we shall see, had no expectation of a military victory against Prussia, limited or otherwise. Second, we have every reason to believe that Dr. Conneau would quite willingly have misled the empress if asked to do so. He did not like her, but was well known for his absolute loyalty to Napoleon. A better conjecture than Dr. Witkowski's is that Dr. Conneau informed Napoleon of the contents of Sée's case-report "as the one who had the right to see it," and that the emperor himself, considering the new crisis brewing over the Hohenzollern candidacy, preferred secrecy for the moment. He had kept many secrets from the empress before, and her by then well-known penchant for chattering to the Austrian ambassador would hardly have inclined the emperor to trust her at a critical moment with the news from Dr. Sée. It is of course possible that Conneau, supported by Corvisart, softened the impact of Dr. Sée's diagnosis by telling the emperor of the divided opinion at the consultation. But there can be no doubt that the emperor knew himself to be far from well, whatever the cause. In recalling the aged Marshal Randon to active duty to take over the government of Algeria during the crisis, the emperor admitted to Randon that he also was too old for the campaign against Prussia. A sadness crept over his face, he seemed weighed down with apprehension, and then added: "I am not at all well." Randon was deeply struck by the interview.[24]

Historians today do not believe that the Hohenzollern candidacy for the Spanish throne was engineered by Bismarck as a further insult to the French designed to draw them into war. Rather, they think that he favored that

[24] Comte J.-L.-C.-A. Randon, *Mémoires du maréchal Randon*, Paris: Lahure, 1875-1877, II, 308.

candidacy when it became a possibility and saw the opportunity to create a European crisis out of it.[25] The liberal French government throughout the crisis in July, conscious of the humiliation of 1867 and determined to present itself as no less patriotic than its conservative Bonapartist opponents, fell into Bismarck's trap through a series of inept responses to the crisis. Ultimately declaring war against Prussia, the French government seemed to be the aggressor and went to war without foreign sympathy or ally. German documents published in 1957 have made it quite clear that not only was Napoleon opposed to a war, but that the Hohenzollerns knew it.[26] Napoleon was not opposed to the Hohenzollerns as a dynasty and pointed out that Prince Leopold, the Hohenzollern in question, was a great-grandson of Caroline Bonaparte and a grandson of Stéphanie Beauharnais, more recently related to these French families than to the Prussian Hohenzollerns. What Napoleon feared was that no foreign prince could successfully reign in Spain, and that within several years Prussia would have an excuse to come to Leopold's aid. In that case, the French would be faced with a situation reminiscent of the Hapsburg encirclement of the sixteenth century.[27]

When French diplomacy secured Prince Leopold's

[25] Lawrence D. Steefel, *Bismarck, the Hohenzollern Candidacy and the Origins of the Franco-Prussian War of 1870*, Cambridge: Harvard University Press, 1962, p. 244.

[26] *Georges Bonnin, Bismarck and the Hohenzollern Candidature for the Spanish Throne*, London: Chatto & Windus, 1957, p. 250.

[27] A. Mels, *Wilhelmshoehe, souvenirs de la captivité de Napoléon III*, Paris: Dupont, 1880, pp. 58-59.

withdrawal from candidacy, which the emperor several times said would be sufficient to avoid war,[28] the crisis should have been over. But the resentments bred in 1867 bore results for Bismarck, as French patriotic sentiments led the government to strain for an even greater diplomatic victory and gave Bismarck a last opportunity to construct a new insult, the famous Ems Despatch, which he himself called a red rag for the Gallic bull. In 1910, a retired French bureaucrat who was an ardent patriot published as fact a rumor that had long been current to the effect that on the night of July 14, 1870, when the French cabinet was considering what response to make to the Ems Despatch, the emperor suffered a spell of faintness and left the room to revive. At the moment of his departure, the ministers were considering a proposal to call for a European Congress to settle the crisis, a proposal the emperor favored.

In his absence, a matter of thirty or forty-five minutes, as this version would have it, the empress, learning of the pacific bent of the discussion, came into the council room and obtained a vote for war.[29] We are to understand from this that when the emperor returned to the council room his government was too committed to war for a reversal and, furthermore, that his momentary ill-health had made the difference between peace and war. That the empress was a militant voice there can be no doubt, but the history of their marital relationship makes it absurd to suppose that Napoleon would have allowed himself to be overruled by his wife on such a momentous issue.

[28] Bonnin, *op. cit.*, pp. 257-258; and La Gorce, *op. cit.*, vi, 265.

[29] Henri Welschinger, *La Guerre de 1870, causes et responsabilités*, Paris: Plon-Nourrit, 1910, i, 153-155.

Moreover, even under the Liberal Empire he retained sufficient executive authority to sway his ministers, and a vote for war meant that he had given his approval, however reluctantly.

For all Emile Ollivier's dislike of the empress (and he was the minister who proposed to call a European Congress), for all his dedication after 1870 to proving that Napoleon and the Liberal Empire had not been responsible for the war of 1870, he never buttressed his defense with the story of the fainting spell. In the fourteenth volume of his massive apologia, published the year before the Welschinger book, Ollivier made no mention of any fainting spell on the night of July 14; certainly he would have mentioned it had it taken place as a vindication of his esteemed emperor.[30] Ollivier produced an abridged edition of his eighteen-volume work several years later, and here he specifically denied that the famous incident had taken place.[31]

Ollivier's attempt to set the record straight must not be attributed to any special pleading for the empress. Indeed, one of his bitterest memories was of a lunch when Madame Walewska "turned her back on us and the empress pretended not to see us because we were ready to accept the [Hohenzollern] renunciation."[32] Neither Napoleon nor Ollivier wanted war, but both of them gave in to the pressure of public opinion, something difficult

[30] Emile Ollivier, *L'Empire libéral; études, récits, souvenirs*, Paris: Garnier frères, 1897-1918 (Vol. XIV in 1909).

[31] Emile Ollivier, *The Franco-Prussian War and its Hidden Causes*, Boston: Little, Brown, 1914, pp. 328-329.

[32] Emile Ollivier, *Lettres de l'exil, 1870-1874*, Paris: Hachette, 1921, p. 23, Ollivier to the Duc de Gramont, Jan. 17, 1871.

to escape in a government based on universal suffrage. To have accepted the affront offered by Prussia would have meant a loss of honor, a greater national disaster in the long run than military defeat.[33] The emperor was in a poor position to resist the public pressure and that of the conservative Bonapartists "because of his line at the time of Sadowa, and [he] could not afford the appearance of 'truckling' to Prussia."[34]

The imperial court had taken up summer residence at Saint-Cloud on June 7, 1870. There it was that the emperor first saw Dr. Sée on June 19, and war was declared exactly one month later. When it was announced that the emperor would take supreme command, the faithful Princess Mathilde, horrified by his appearance, told him emphatically that he was in no condition to join the army. His answer to her: "You exaggerate, my dear, . . . you exaggerate." He seemed resigned to his fate.[35] Marshal Bazaine had expected to be given the supreme command, and his appointment would have been shrewd for a number of reasons. Bazaine, as a commoner risen to the highest rank, was a favorite of the left-wing opposition, and his nomination could have solidified the home front. As Napoleon knew that the army was unprepared and that he had no alliance to redress the balance, he could have avoided committing his dynastic prestige by remaining in Paris. His health alone would have been sufficient reason. Instead, he did what he thought was his duty. He knew

[33] *Ibid.*, p. 93, Ollivier to the Comtesse de Magnac, Nov. 27, 1871.

[34] Lord Newton, *op. cit.*, I, 301-302, Lord Lyons to Lord Granville, July 19, 1870.

[35] Paléologue, *op. cit.*, pp. 141-142.

that his corps commanders had been given to bickering and perhaps suspected that only an emperor's orders could produce the necessary unity of command;[36] possibly, too, his superstitious nature spurred him toward a tragic fate.

His departure for the front on July 28 was a solemn affair with none of the hysterical enthusiasm seen in Paris as the troops were mobilized. Many members of the court were reluctant to see the emperor leave, knowing him to be unwell, but since virtually none of them knew his true condition, they did not know how absolutely unfit he was for a campaign.[37] Probably most of the courtiers accepted the emperor's idea that he belonged at the head of his army, if doubting that it was necessary or proper to take along the fourteen-year-old prince imperial.[38] When the emperor's party had boarded the train, the emperor looked out upon the waiting court. Suddenly he caught sight of one of the chamberlains and called out, "Beaumanoir, I forgot to say goodbye to you!" They were his last words as the train steamed out. The empress called after them, "Do your duty, Louis!" leaving the court to wonder which Louis she had meant: father or son?[39]

In addition to several valets de chambre, the emperor's party included eight aides-de-camp (Generals Edgar Ney, Lebrun, Castelnau, Yvelin de Beville, Waubert de Genlis,

[36] Fernand Giraudeau, *Napoléon III intime*, Paris: Paul Ollendorff, 1895, pp. 409-410.

[37] Dr. Thomas W. Evans, *The Second French Empire*, New York: D. Appleton, 1905, p. 489.

[38] Comtesse Stéphanie de Tascher de la Pagerie, *Mon séjour aux Tuileries*, Paris: Paul Ollendorff, 1893, III, 212.

[39] Commandant Schneider, *Le Second Empire à Saint-Cloud*, Paris: Victor-Havard, 1894, p. 18.

Reille, Favé, and Pajol), several of whom left accounts of the campaign. There were also eight ordnance officers, an adjutant, a map officer, and several secretaries headed by Franceschini Piétri. Colonel Jacques-Albert Verly commanded the personal escort, the Cent-Gardes. The medical service comprised Doctors Conneau and Corvisart, augmented by a young surgeon, Dr. Théophile Anger,[40] who was a former student of Nélaton and whose presence suggests that Dr. Nélaton in fact knew what the emperor's trouble was.

The emperor reached Metz the day after leaving Saint-Cloud and wrote the empress-regent a brief note that reeked of weariness, his last sentence concluding, "provided that my health and my strength hold up!"[41] The first minor military engagement took place at Saarbrük on August 2, and after it the emperor dismounted and began walking toward his carriage, supporting himself on General Lebrun's arm. When asked if he were in pain, the emperor admitted that he was suffering terribly. Lebrun suggested that they summon the carriage, but the emperor said that he preferred to walk a bit.[42] No doubt there were medical reasons for his anguish, but what he had found upon reaching the front confirmed his worst suspicions about the lack of military preparation for a campaign. "Nothing is ready," he wrote the empress from

[40] Germain Bapst, *Le Maréchal Canrobert. Souvenirs d'un siècle*, Paris: Plon, 1903-1904, IV, 386-387; and Baron Albert Verly, *Souvenirs du Second Empire: les étapes douloureuses (l'empereur de Metz à Sedan)*, Paris: Daragon, 1908, p. 238.

[41] "Lettres à l'impératrice Eugénie," *Revue des deux mondes*, LIX (September 1, 1930), 6.

[42] General B.-L.-J. Lebrun, *Souvenirs militaires, 1866-1870*, Paris: E. Dentu, 1895, p. 223.

Forbach. "We do not have sufficient troops. I regard us already as lost."[43] His pessimism may have been justified, but it should have led him to give up the command at once to someone more optimistic and energetic. When the empress received that despatch, she showed it to Prince Metternich, an astonishing move considering that the French still hoped to obtain Austrian intervention.

By August 7 the emperor did begin to consider relinquishing supreme command. After the initial defeats in Alsace, a general retreat began, Marshal MacMahon's forces retiring upon the Camp de Châlons, while Marshal Bazaine backed into the shelter of Metz. Napoleon was with Marshal MacMahon, and they expected to find reserves and to regroup on reaching Châlons. The question of the emperor's giving up supreme command in the field was more a reflection of a political situation, however, than a military matter. The initial reverses had led the Republican opposition in Paris to make demands upon the empress that threatened her authority, and a number of the generals, aware that they could spare the emperor from the front, urged him to return to the headship of government. He had a popularity that the empress did not enjoy and was needed to rally the home front. Accordingly, the supreme command in the field was conferred upon Marshal Bazaine on August 12, perhaps a popular decision, but a choice that was to prove to be disastrous.[44]

Soon after, Napoleon told Marshal MacMahon of his decision to return to Paris; the two of them believed that,

[43] Pauline Metternich-Winneburg, *Souvenirs de la princesse Pauline de Metternich 1859-1871*, Paris: Plon-Nourrit, 1922, p. 197.

[44] Lebrun, *op. cit.*, pp. 280-298.

with Bazaine cornered in Metz, the wisest strategy would be for MacMahon to retire on Paris to help with the defense of the city. When these decisions were transmitted to the government in Paris, the empress and her new minister of war (the liberal regime had been turned out after the initial defeats) telegraphed back that for political reasons Marshal Bazaine must be rescued and that the emperor must not return to Paris without a victory. Knowing conditions in Paris only second-hand, the emperor gave way and told MacMahon that he would remain with the army for the time being but would not interfere. MacMahon had to decide whether to move in the direction of Paris as planned or to move toward the rescue of Bazaine as instructed from Paris. In the end he decided to obey instructions even though he knew the emperor disapproved of the maneuver and even though his communications with Bazaine were sufficiently slim as to preclude effective cooperation of the two armies. We cannot know whether the Parisians would have refused to defend the capital if Bazaine had been abandoned to Prussian siege in Metz as the government feared, though it seems far-fetched considering Parisian patriotism; we do know that the movement toward Metz set the scene for military disaster.[45]

The emperor's situation was made ludicrous by these decisions. No longer commanding, he became an annoying obstruction on the march, with his baggage train and his young son, once MacMahon began moving in the di-

[45] Deposition of Marshal MacMahon, *Enquête parlementaire sur le gouvernement de la défense nationale*, Paris and Versailles, 1872-1875, I, 29-32; and Léon Laforge, *Histoire complète de MacMahon*, Paris: Lamulle & Poisson, 1898, I, 248, 268.

rection of Metz. General officers resented his presence as a handicap, for it was difficult for others to command with him on the scene, and in the anxiety of defeat they found him as a nonprofessional an easy scapegoat. Mortally wounded, General Decaen sneered at him as an "imbecile who involves himself in commanding and who understands nothing about it."[46] Certainly Napoleon belonged back in Paris, if for no other reason than that of health. As they moved northward he had frequent seizures of pain and once blurted out to General Prince de la Moskowa, "Ah! if I could just die!"[47] His aides were aware of his great pain but, not knowing the cause, supposed that it was neuralgia.[48] The empress, though under no illusions about the desperate military situation, believed that the emperor was actually bearing up very well.[49] In *La Débâcle*, Emile Zola portrayed the emperor on campaign as rouged like an actor. Zola is believable, because cosmetics had undoubtedly been used earlier in Paris. Photographs exist which make it quite plain that the emperor had often been made-up to appear younger and well for public occasions. But eyewitnesses on the campaign make it equally clear that he had a ravaged appearance, that he was aged and suffering.[50]

[46] Paul Guériot, *La Captivité de Napoléon III en Allemagne*, Paris: Perrin, 1926, pp. 2-3.

[47] La Gorce, *op. cit.*, VII, 250.

[48] General Henri Castelnau, "Sedan et Wilhelmshöhe" (Journal du Général Castelnau, aide de camp de Napoléon III), Louis Sonolet, ed., *la Revue de Paris*, XXXVI (Oct. 1, 1929), p. 513.

[49] Mérimée, *op. cit.*, XV, 157-158, Mérimée to Mme. de Montijo, August 24, 1870.

[50] Guériot, *op. cit.*, p. 245.

The forces that Marshal MacMahon led to the aid of Bazaine were very inferior in discipline, morale, and numbers to the army in Metz they were meant to rescue. Moving slowly and without adequate information about enemy strength and position, MacMahon soon found himself outmaneuvered and greatly outnumbered, making the immediate relief of Bazaine impossible and leading to a retreat upon Sedan. Even though French headquarters was to be established in the village of Carignan, some distance from Sedan, the ranking generals wanted to send Napoleon on to Mézières, roughly twenty kilometers west of Sedan. There he would not only evade capture in case of disaster at Sedan, but from there he could join Vinoy's XIII Corps, which was known to be approaching from that side to give MacMahon reinforcement. The prince imperial was sent to safety, but the emperor refused to go. He said that he did not want to threaten morale by leaving at the supreme moment in the struggle, and he insisted that he must share the fate of the army.[51]

The battle of Sedan began about five in the morning on September 1, and the French were soon boxed-in and outgunned. Napoleon got on horseback and rode in the direction of Bazeilles, where the fighting was heaviest. Within an hour he met Marshal MacMahon, already wounded and out of action, being taken to shelter. The command at once devolved upon General Ducrot, but General Wimpffen had been supplied with a secret letter from the ministry of war in Paris giving him command in the event of MacMahon's incapacity. The demoralized

[51] General Comte C.-P.-Victor Pajol, *Lettre de M. le général Pajol sur la capitulation de Sedan*, Paris: Lefebvre, 1871, pp. 4-6.

MacMahon had done little to prepare either to retreat from Sedan or to link up with Vinoy in the west, whereas Ducrot almost immediately began to give orders to remove the army from the hopeless trap that Sedan was. Wimpffen did not assert himself until he got word of the impending westward retreat, whereupon he gave countermanding orders that brought a fatal chaos to the defense.

Napoleon, meanwhile, spent a half-hour in the midst of a division of marines defending Bazeilles, and all witnesses testified that he repeatedly and needlessly exposed himself to enemy fire, seeking a death that would not come.[52] As the morning developed and the emperor moved to different sectors, he was several times obliged to get off his horse and walk because of his pain.[53] Toward eleven o'clock he met General Wimpffen, who told him not to worry—that he would throw the enemy into the Meuse within two hours—but the emperor was not long in recognizing the real extent of the disaster. Wimpffen was determined to break out of the city on the eastern side in order to conform to his secret instructions to move toward Metz, and a brief French counterattack on that side encouraged him to believe that the way was open, which in fact it was not. Consequently Wimpffen was dismayed to learn that the emperor toward midafternoon had intervened by ordering a white flag to be raised from the top of the citadel. He was asserting his right as sovereign, not as commander of the besieged army, and he

[52] *Ibid.*, pp. 8-11; and l'Abbé Eugène Lanusse, *Sedan, l'heure suprême*, Paris: Flammarion, 1892, pp. 306-308.

[53] General Prince de la Moskowa, "Quelques notes intimes sur la guerre de 1870," *le Correspondant*, Dec. 10, 1898, pp. 969-970; and Castelnau, *op. cit.* (Oct. 15, 1929), p. 852.

thought that by surrendering himself he could obtain the best terms for the army and for France.[54]

On the following day, September 2, 1870, Wimpffen had to accept terms for the unconditional surrender of the army, which passed into captivity. Napoleon, also to be a prisoner, waited in the Chateau de Belle Vue for the king of Prussia and the final ceremonies. While waiting he read from a book in the chateau library, and when the king arrived the emperor turned down the corner of the page and put the book aside. A Bavarian officer noted the page and discovered that the emperor had underlined a passage he had been reading; the officer gave the volume to R. H. Armit, a war correspondent for the Manchester *Guardian*, who had been covering the war from the Prussian headquarters.

The volume was an 1831 edition of the *Essays* of Montaigne, and the underlined section was Montaigne's commentary on Cicero's views on the immortality of the soul:

> Two things make this belief plausible: For one thing, without the immortality of souls, there would be no way to judge presumptious aspirations for greatness, which is one mark of great success in this world. In the second place, they provide a useful record, as Plato said, so that when vices have been hidden from the sight and knowledge of human justice, they shall always remain exposed to divine [justice] which will punish them, even after the death of the guilty. Man takes great pains to prolong his existence; . . . for the preservation of the body there is the tomb; but fame

[54] Pajol, *op. cit.*, pp. 12-13; and Lebrun, *Bazeilles-Sedan*, Paris: E. Dentu, 1891, p. 130.

> provides for the preservation of a man's name. He exerts his entire mind to recasting himself, impatient as he is with his lot, and to shoring himself up with his contrivances.

Mr. Armit took the book back to England, jotted down its history on the flyleaf, and ultimately presented it to N.W.J. Strode, the owner of Camden House in Chislehurst.[55]

The king of Prussia selected Wilhelmshöhe, a chateau near Cassel, as Napoleon's residence during his detention. It had once been the palace of his uncle, the late King Jerome of Westphalia, at which time it had been called Napoleonshöhe. This will account for the presence of the portrait of Queen Hortense which Napoleon III met unexpectedly on his first tour of the building. He was so startled and moved by the encounter that he asked the entourage to leave him temporarily. As he himself put it, he had found his mother there waiting for him.[56] The Prussian king gave instructions that the emperor was to be well treated, and that the public was to be kept away from the railroad stations in the proximity of Wilhelmshöhe. At the time, the officials in charge of the emperor thought that the instructions were meant to spare the emperor hostile demonstrations, but they came to realize that the Prussians also feared the possibility of anti-Prussian demonstrations in that section of Germany.

The emperor's warden at Wilhelmshöhe was General

[55] Sir William Fraser, *Napoleon III (My Recollections)*, London: Sampson, Low, Marston, 1896, pp. 207-210.

[56] Comtesse Louise de Mercy-Argenteau, *The Last Love of an Emperor*, London: Iris, 1916, p. 231.

Count Karl von Monts, a man who shared the view of most Prussian officers that the emperor ought to be treated as a criminal responsible for the war. But Monts obeyed his king's orders and in his daily visits with the emperor came to like him, giving us by far the best description we have of Napoleon during those months after Sedan. He was impressed by Napoleon's command of the German language, not simply his extensive vocabulary, but the nuances of German, which greatly facilitated their communication even though the emperor generally preferred to converse in French.[57]

The emperor's reserve set the tone for his entire staff at Wilhelmshöhe. He was invariably calm and never gave way to outbursts of spite or despair, never even complaining about the conduct of his former marshals, so that he created the impression of a man of great internal strength. Throughout his captivity he was constantly occupied with study and writing (prison had been his only university) and he gave the impression of a man who had a real love for work. German military institutions were his primary interest during those months. Monts thought that the emperor was notably superior in mind and education to all the men in his entourage, though he also had a high opinion of Generals Castelnau and Pajol. By the end of the captivity, Monts no longer saw the emperor as a criminal, but as a humanitarian, a good man who had given in to political pressures that he ought to have resisted.[58]

When General von Monts prepared his memoirs for publication, he knew not only the rumors of Napoleon's

[57] General von Monts, *La Captivité de Napoléon en Allemagne*, Paris: Pierre Lafitte, 1910, pp. 2-14.

[58] *Ibid.*, pp. 33-53.

ill-health but the apparent cause of his death. Yet Monts insisted that the emperor had showed no signs of a bladder stone while at Wilhelmshöhe. He suffered continually from a nasal catarrh, but that seemed almost normal for a man of his age as colder, damper weather came on. For exercise and pleasure he several times rode horseback and remained in the saddle for more than two hours at a stretch.[59] The period at Wilhelmshöhe was the third apparent recovery from the symptoms of a calculus and helps us to understand why Doctors Conneau and Corvisart, both present at Wilhelmshöhe, might feel assured that Dr. Sée's diagnosis had been wrong. What is more, they did not believe that anyone with such an agonizing malady could have performed as well as he had.[60] Perhaps they were rationalizing their uncertainty or their inaction in July, but the recovery was encouraging. In October, we hear that the emperor was experiencing a minor attack of gout that kept him indoors;[61] but when the emperor wrote to the empress on December 19 that his health was better and that his strength was reviving,[62] he confirmed Monts's observations.

Meanwhile, the emperor had to prepare to live outside prison, for his captivity was not to be permanent. On several occasions he was visited by his private treasurer, Charles Thélin, so that he did have a general notion of his financial resources. An old Italian friend, Count Arese, grateful for what Napoleon had done for Italy, was fear-

[59] *Ibid.*, pp. 120-121, 263.

[60] Fernand Giraudeau, *La Mort et les funérailles de Napoléon III*, Paris: Amyot, 1873, p. 7.

[61] Castelnau, *op. cit.* (Nov. 1, 1929), p. 184.

[62] "Lettres à l'impératrice Eugénie," *op. cit.*, p. 20, Napoleon III to Eugénie, Dec. 19, 1870.

ful that the emperor would be the victim of total confiscation and put himself at the emperor's service. Napoleon wrote to Arese on November 14, 1870, to assure him that for the moment neither he nor the empress was in difficulty. (The empress had been spirited out of Paris by Napoleon's American dentist, Dr. Evans, and had taken up residence in England.) They did not have the millions popularly attributed to them, but did have enough cash to maintain themselves comfortably for about a year. For the future, the empress had jewels that could be sold, and he had inherited, as well as bought, properties in Italy that should produce income adequate for them to live like good bourgeois.

Count Arese assumed the management of the inherited properties in the Romagna, in the Marches, and in Friuli, in the interest of income managing them more efficiently than they had been looked after previously. But the Italian property that Napoleon had purchased, the Farnese Palace, was another matter. He had bought it in a state of disrepair from Francis II of Naples after that monarch had been dislodged from his throne by Garibaldi and needed money. Not only had the adjacent gardens and land brought in no income, but Napoleon had begun a substantial investment in the property to restore the palace. Arese felt that this property must be sold, but Napoleon was reluctant to sell if the sale would compromise the restoration, which he saw as an important contribution to scholars and archeologists. As a result, Arese made an arrangement with the Italian government to purchase the property for less than the million francs he thought it was worth, with the understanding that the Italians would continue the restoration. Napoleon received 250,000 francs for the property and 400,000 francs for the improvements he had made.[63] It meant, as Napoleon said, a comfortable income for the remainder of their lives, though strict economy had to be practiced to maintain the small court that gathered in exile. When Napoleon was released from Wilhelmshöhe in the spring of 1871 after the Germans made peace with the new French government, he joined the empress in Chislehurst, just southeast of London, in Kent. They had rented Camden Place, a house built in 1609. Most members of the entourage received only a fraction of their former salaries, and those with private means usually received nothing.[64]

Reports from Chislehurst that the emperor was in good health during 1871 and into 1872 were not disingenuous, though they were suspect as an attempt to provide proof that the emperor was fit to resume the throne. Members of the entourage passed back and forth between Britain and France, always under police surveillance, and Dr. Conneau was notably active in drumming up Bonapartist support. On the other hand, he also reported that the political disagreements between emperor and empress continued, suggesting that there were no real plans to attempt a coup d'état.[65] Visitors to Camden Place as late as July of 1872 were struck both by the emperor's good health and by his lack of bitterness,[66] but the old urinary symp-

[63] Count Giuseppe Grabinski, *Un Ami de Napoléon III. Le comte Arese et la politique italienne sous le second empire*, Paris: Bahl, 1897, pp. 243-251.

[64] Police dossier, B a/1.019.

[65] Police dossier, B a/1.017.

[66] Evariste Bavoux, *Chislehurst. Tuileries, souvenirs intimes sur l'empereur*, Paris: E. Dentu, 1873, pp. 9-23.

toms began to reappear by the summer of that year. First Corvisart and then Conneau became convinced that Dr. Sée had probably been right in his diagnosis of July, 1870.[67] They decided to call in Sir Henry Thompson, a specialist in genito-urinary surgery.

Sir Henry, who had been trained at University College, London, had also studied the methods of Dr. Civiale in Paris, the surgeon who had developed the method of crushing bladder stones with a lithotrite. Civiale's method involved crushing at repeated sessions, allowing the patient to void the fragments. Thompson later tried to improve upon Civiale's method, completing the crushing and the removal of the fragments in one session by using a more powerful lithotrite, a large evacuating catheter, and a suction device developed for the operation. The use of an anesthetic permitted the more lengthy procedure. Thompson was knighted after his successful operation on Leopold I of Belgium in 1863, using his new method. He was also known as a painter, a novelist, an astronomer, a collector of Nanking china, a champion of cremation, and a giver of celebrated dinners, surely an eminent Victorian.[68]

On July 19, 1872, he listened to the history of the emperor's case and conducted his examination. He learned that the hemorrhoids dated from Ham, but that they had been particularly troublesome since 1866, and that the emperor was always in more difficulty when cold weather came. He knew of the probing at Vichy and the pain and subsequent fever, and that now in 1872 Napoleon was

[67] Giraudeau, *op. cit.*, pp. 7-10.

[68] Dr. S. F. Marwood, "Louis Napoleon and his Doctors," *Medical Journal of the Southwest*, LXXXII (January 1967), 77-78.

suffering from pains in the region of the anus and the perineum. By rectal examination Thompson found much "thickening and prolapsus all round." But the prostate seemed to be normal. Conneau and Corvisart agreed with Thompson that at least a soft catheter ought to be used to examine the bladder, but the emperor refused to submit. Nor would he agree to take any opiates to ease his pain, saying that they did not agree with him. He was told that he must eat green vegetables more frequently and that hot bran bags placed locally would help to relieve his pain.[69]

When Dr. Evans, the American dentist, called professionally at Camden Place in October of 1872, the emperor told him that he thought it was again time to consult a British physician. Evans recommended that he see Sir James Paget, and Napoleon said that he would be grateful if Evans would make the necessary arrangements. Sir James went down to Chislehurst on October 31 and found his friend Sir William Gull already there. Gull had been appointed physician to the Prince of Wales in 1871 and had been created a baronet in recognition of his services during the prince's illness that year. His presence at Camden Place was a measure of the royal family's concern. Unfortunately, Gull had an imperious manner and a dogmatic personality (which would later bear upon this case), rendering him unpopular and leaving him open to much criticism, whereas Paget was a modest, retiring man who enjoyed the biggest surgical practice in London in his day. The two men were congenial, however, and

[69] From Thompson's notebook, in Sir Zachary Cope, *The Versatile Victorian: Being the Life of Sir Henry Thompson*, London: Harvey and Blythe, 1951, pp. 55-56.

joined Conneau and Corvisart in a consultation. Paget thought that the trouble had to do with a bladder irritation, and that this might be due to a calculus. On the other hand, he found that "the usual signs of calculus were not well-marked."[70] For the moment, therefore, an operation was not prescribed, in the hope that a proper regimen and rest would make it possible for the emperor to live, though with pain.[71]

Baron Beust was one of the visitors to Chislehurst who thought that the emperor submitted to medical examination only because he expected to have to show himself soon in public on horseback—that a second return from Elba was in preparation.[72] But Beust was an embittered man by then, bearing a grudge against the Bonapartes, and was an unreliable witness.[73] In contrast, Dr. Conneau, an enthusiast for that presumed return from Elba, had become quite discouraged before the end of 1872. The emperor seemed to have no plans and had told Conneau that it would be necessary to let matters develop indefinitely.[74] In any case the emperor believed that a restoration was not possible through a coup d'état but would require the mandate of universal suffrage.[75]

The emperor's condition grew worse during November and December, and on the twenty-fourth Thompson,

[70] Evans Collection, Thomas W. Evans Dental Museum, University of Pennsylvania: Envelope #34 (Black Box Collection), Paget to Evans, January 7, 1873.

[71] Dr. Evans, *op. cit.*, pp. 490-491.

[72] Beust, *Memoirs*, London: Remington, 1887, II, 195.

[73] Particularly evident in Beust's *Le Dernier des Napoléon*, Paris: Lacroix, Verboeckoven, 1872.

[74] Police dossier, B a/1.107.

[75] Evans, *op. cit.*, p. 493.

Paget, and Gull were recalled for further consultation. Whereas previously blood had appeared in the urine only after exercise in the saddle, now it appeared after any exercise. The pain was now chiefly perineal. Napoleon agreed to allow Thompson to pass a soft catheter to see if the bladder could evacuate its contents, which it did nearly completely. *All* the physicians present told the emperor that it was absolutely essential that he be sounded, under chloroform, to determine once and for all whether a stone was present, and he soon consented.[76] This exploration took place on December 26, the anesthetic being administered by Mr. Clover, the most accomplished chloroformist of that day. The emperor took the anesthetic well. Sir Henry Thompson performed the sounding and found a stone "not less than that of a full-sized date" in the bladder.

Thompson believed that a crushing operation, given the age and health of the patient, was preferable to any form of lithotomy. Paget agreed, especially considering that Thompson's skill in lithotrity was then unequaled in Britain. Doctors Conneau and Corvisart were made responsible for preparing facilities for the operation, and Thompson took up residence at Camden Place on December 30 in order to observe the imperial patient's condition and habits. Napoleon then confessed to Sir Henry how severely he had suffered on the day of Sedan, from which Sir Henry inferred that the emperor really had sought death in battle. He also noticed that the emperor's heavy cigarette-smoking seemed to afford him some alleviation from pain and weariness.[77]

[76] Evans Collection, *ibid.*, Paget to Evans, Jan. 7, 1873.

[77] Cope, *op. cit.*, p. 57.

Even though Thompson preferred to complete an operation in one session, the condition of his patient suggested Civiale's older method of briefer, repeated sessions. The first operation was scheduled for 3:30 P.M. on January 2, 1873. Present were Thompson, his assistant John Foster, Gull, Conneau, Corvisart, and Clover. The emperor again took the anesthetic easily, whereupon Thompson took a flat-bladed lithotrite and seized the calculus with no difficulty. Its friability indicated that it was chiefly phosphatic, easily crushed, but the type of calculus especially apt to recur.[78] Thompson was able to remove considerable debris after three or four introductions, and there was only a trace of blood. The emperor's recovery of consciousness was normal, though early in the evening he experienced a slight shiver. But this, as Thompson later explained, was then "a very common occurrence after lithotrity, before the necessity for complete sterilization of all lithotrites and other instruments employed . . . was known or practised."[79]

Thompson was not optimistic after the first operation. The urine was alkaline, thick and cloudy with pus and mucus and with crystals of phosphate, though no other deviations from the natural standard of urine were noted.[80] Furthermore, the stone was so large and the emperor so unusually sensitive and difficult to manage, that Thompson reported his anxiety to the Prince of Wales and warned that he might fail.[81] Considering the size of

[78] Evans Collection, *ibid.*, Paget to Evans, Jan. 7, 1873.

[79] Cope, *op. cit.*, p. 59.

[80] *Lancet*, I (January 11, 1873), 58.

[81] Ivor Guest, *Napoleon III in England*, London: British Technical and General Press, 1952, p. 194.

the stone, Thompson also exclaimed to those at Camden House, "What extraordinary heroism the emperor must have possessed, to sit in his saddle for five hours, holding on with both hands, during the battle of Sedan! The agony must have been constant. I cannot understand how he could have borne it."[82] Thompson had, in fact, never known anything to equal it.

On January 3 and 4, the urine seemed to contain an increasing proportion of blood, making Thompson suspect that a fragment of stone had been caught in the neck of the bladder and requiring a second operation sooner than he would have liked. It was arranged for Monday, January 6. Just before the chloroform was to be administered, the emperor suffered a second seizure of severe shivering, and the operation was postponed for two hours until he had apparently recovered. Then Thompson proceeded and found the expected fragment in the bladder neck, crushing it and permitting the removal of the debris.

On the following day the urine was more bloody and urination more frequent. The emperor seemed sleepy and was often incoherent. Dr. Gull thought that this sleepiness was natural, but Thompson feared that it might signify uremic poisoning. On the eighth his condition seemed unchanged except for signs that another crushed fragment might be blocking the bladder neck, and a third operation was therefore scheduled for January 9. At six that morning, the patient seemed improved, giving reason for encouragement. But at 10:25 A.M., when Thompson, Conneau, and Corvisart returned to the bedroom they found at once a change in appearance and

[82] Evans, *op. cit.*, p. 494; and Alfred Comte de La Chapelle, *Oeuvres posthumes et autographes inédits de Napoléon III en exil*, Paris: Lachaud, 1873, pp. 247-248.

pulse and knew that he was lost. His last mumbled words were for the loyal Dr. Conneau, recalling that they had been at Sedan together. Death, which had disdained him there, came quietly to claim him at 10:45.[83]

His face in death was notably serene. The features were molded that evening by Brucciani of the Royal Academy in preparation for a bust. On the tenth, Dr. Thompson sketched the emperor's head, and photographs were taken.[84] Napoleon III had won a certain popularity in England as a former ally and a gracious guest of the country, and many English came to Chislehurst for the funeral. Delegations from all walks of French life crossed the Channel to attend, and it was estimated that three thousand people followed the hearse, many of whom did not have opportunity to sign the official register.[85] Canrobert and Leboeuf, his former marshals, both attended, Leboeuf weeping bitterly at the sight of the body. Marshal MacMahon, created both a duke and a marshal by Napoleon after a victory that some thought belonged more to the emperor than to MacMahon,[86] failed to appear. His absence was resented by loyal Bonapartists.[87]

A mortuary chapel attached to the local church of St.

[83] Cope, *op. cit.*, pp. 59-61; and *Lancet*, I (Jan. 11, 1873), 59-60.

[84] Francis Aubert, *Le Journal du Chislehurst, du 9 au 17 janvier 1873*, Paris: Lachaud, 1873, p. 13.

[85] In the Duc M.-J.-P. de Cambacérès, *Funérailles de Napoléon III*, Paris: Librairie Générale, 1873, one can find both the details of the funeral and the alphabetical list of those who signed the register at Camden Place.

[86] General Comte Fleury, *Souvenirs*, Paris: Plon, Nourrit, 1897-1898, II, 45.

[87] Fernand Giraudeau, a former official in the ministry of the interior, also left a brief account: *La Mort et les funérailles de Napoléon III*, Paris: Amyot, 1873.

Mary was built to receive the emperor's body, where it was joined in 1879 by that of the prince imperial, killed in Africa fighting for the British army. The Empress Eugénie then wished to build a new mausoleum near the church but was unable to purchase the necessary land. In 1881 she moved to Farnborough Hill in Hampshire, giving its Church and Abbey of St. Michael to the Benedictines. Seven years later, in 1888, the bodies of her husband and son were removed to a memorial chapel at Farnborough, where they yet remain. No subsequent French regime has seriously considered returning him to the banks of the Seine, to the Paris that was the work of the Second Empire.

There is no error so monstrous that it fails to find defenders among the ablest men.

Lord Acton

6 *The Case Revisited*

The post-mortem examination took place on Friday afternoon, January 10, 1873, in the presence of Doctors Thompson, Gull, Conneau, and Corvisart. For the pathologist they chose the most distinguished specialist available, Professor John S. Burdon-Sanderson of University College, London. The results were published in the London *Times* the following day as well as in *Lancet*:

> The kidneys were found to be involved in the inflammatory effects produced by the irritation of the vesical

calculus (which must have been in the bladder several years) to a degree which was not suspected; and if it had been suspected could not have been ascertained. The disease of the kidneys was of two kinds: There was on the one hand dilation of both ureters and of the pelves of the kidneys. On the left side the dilation was excessive, and had given rise to atrophy of the glandular substance of the organ. On the other, there was sub-acute inflammation of the uriniferous tubes which was of more recent origin. The parts in the neighbourhood of the bladder were in a healthy state. The mucous membrane of the bladder and prostatic urethra exhibited signs of sub-acute inflammation, but not the slightest indication of injury. In the interior of the bladder was found a part of a calculus, the form of which indicated that half had been removed. Besides this there were two or three extremely small fragments, none of them larger than a hemp seed. This half calculus weighed about three-quarters of an ounce, and measured one and a quarter inches by one and five-sixteenths of an inch.

There was no disease of the heart, nor of any other organ excepting the kidneys. The brain and its membranes were in a perfectly natural state. The blood was generally liquid containing only a few small clots. No trace of obstruction by coagula could be found either in the venous system, in the heart, or in the pulmonary artery. Death took place by failure of the circulation, and was attributable to the general constitutional state of the patient. The disease of the kidneys, of which this state was the expression, was of such a nature and so advanced that would in any case have shortly determined a fatal result.[1]

Sir William Gull left the room as soon as the autopsy was completed and did not hear the subsequent discussion of the findings, nor did he sign the report at 6:30 P.M. when the other physicians did. When he did see the report, he declined to sign it, making his own public statement instead.

> I desire to express the opinion that the phosphate of lime calculus which formed the nucleus of the mass was the result of prior cystitis (*catarrhus vesicae*), and not the cause of it. This nucleus was of uncertain duration, and may even have been more recent than supposed in the appended reports. However this may be, it was encrusted by two distinct and more recent formations of crystalline phosphate. The inner incrustration around the amorphous phosphate of lime was dense and separated from the outer incrustation by a looser cellular but crystalline deposit of triple phosphate. It seems to be the judgment more in accordance with clinical experience to regard the cystitis as the prior lesion and that this, by extension, as is common in such cases, affected subsequently the ureters and pelves of the kidneys. No doubt in the later stages of the malady the calculus became, by its formation and increase, an augmenting cause of the lesions. The other facts and statements I entirely endorse.[2]

[1] *Lancet*, 1 (January 1873), 111-112; and Sir Zachary Cope, *The Versatile Victorian: Being the Life of Sir Henry Thompson*, London: Harvey and Blythe, 1951, pp. 61-63.

[2] *Lancet*, 1 (January 1873), 111-112.

What Gull apparently did was to provide additional technical information about the origin and composition of the emperor's bladder stone without really differing from the official report. Yet his independent report, published in the morning papers rather than confined to medical journals, astonished a number of British doctors[3] and won him a rebuke from the editor of *Lancet*.[4] Gull's action, though typical of him and accounting for his unpopularity in the profession, probably encouraged widespread doubt about the reliability of the official report and helped to produce the lengthy medical debate over the emperor's illnesses and death that continued for decades. Gull's report was often called a dissent, although there had been no divided opinion on the part of the physicians present at the autopsy respecting the nature of the case.[5] The Comte de La Chapelle told Edward Legge, a reporter at Chislehurst for the *Morning Post*, that he had overheard Thompson and Gull having a dispute a few hours before the emperor died. Once that rumor was circulated and embroidered, it was only a step to the suspicion that the autopsy report had been drawn up to protect those responsible for the emperor's death and was open to serious doubt.[6] Gull's action also fed this fire. If anything, the official report revealed rather than concealed the physicians' failures.

Gull's statement about the composition of the bladder stone was incorrect. Sir Henry Thompson showed frag-

[3] *Ibid.*, p. 114, J. G. Braden to the Editor.

[4] *Ibid.*, p. 100.

[5] Cope, *op. cit.*, p. 64.

[6] Edward Legge, *The Empress Eugénie 1870-1910*, London: Harper, 1910, p. 77.

ments of the stone to both British and French physicians, including Dr. Debout d'Estrées of the spa at Contrexéville, a specialist in bladder and kidney diseases, and Dr. Ernest Desnos, a well-known urologist. The core of the calculus had been formed of uric acid and urates, the outer layers by phosphates. Both Thompson and Debout thought that the waters of Vichy, particularly alkaline and properly prescribed to neutralize the acid in the urine, were responsible for the beginning of the *outer* layers, and that continual bladder irritation thereafter augmented them. They noted that the more recent of the outer layers were evenly stratified, which they thought reflected the emperor's relaxed existence at Wilhelmshöhe and Chislehurst; earlier layers were irregular and rough, suggesting periods of greater exercise and anxiety.[7] No doubt Dr. Debout was pleased to be able to point an accusing finger at a rival spa, for the waters of Contrexéville, not far from Plombières, presumably restored normal acidity and were prescribed for gravel cases.[8] Ultimately, several physicians practicing in Vichy and resenting the allegations insisted that they had not been grounded in clinical evidence and were mere speculation. Furthermore, they said that the emperor's treatments in Vichy

[7] Dr. Albert-Emile Debout d'Estrées, *Les Causes de la gravelle et de la pierre étudiées à Contrexéville pendant neuf années de pratique médicale*, Paris: Delahaye, 1876, pp. 113-114; Dr. Augustin Cabanès, *Les Morts mystérieuses de l'histoire*, Paris: Michel, 1923-1927, II, 424-425; Sir D'Arcy Power, "Lithotrity: The Case of the Emperor Napoleon III," *The British Journal of Surgery*, XIX, #73 (July 1931), 5.

[8] Dr. Constantin James, *Guide pratique aux eaux minérales de la France et de l'étranger*, Paris: Bloud et Barral, 1896, pp. 199-200.

had been largely limited to bathing in the waters rather than drinking them, since he had gone to Vichy primarily for rheumatism.[9] If so, it would be hard to account for Baron Larrey's insistence in 1865 that the emperor stop going to Vichy, or for Dr. Rayer's request that he leave Vichy at once after the probings by Dr. Guillon in 1866.

Let us assume for the moment, on the basis of the evidence in the autopsy, that Napoleon III died of uremia, an abnormal condition of the blood due to the presence of urea or other urinary substances ordinarily excreted by the kidneys—for the kidneys were impaired and infected—and that in this case, to be more specific, the evidence suggests a chronic latent uremia rather than acute uremia.[10] Second, we may assume also that once the existence of the calculus and its large size had finally been determined it had to be removed by one of several possible methods as it was evidently contributing to bladder neck obstruction, and finally, that the attacks of rigors Napoleon experienced were, as has been noted elsewhere,[11] a response to the severe infection. To these possible points of contention was added a fourth: Should chloroform have been given at all, or was it given excessively?

The first critic of the autopsy, who wrote his quibble

[9] Dr. Pariset, "Quelques notes sur les cures de Napoléon III à Vichy," *la Chronique médicale*, XVII (April 1, 1910), 209-210; and Dr. Gannat, "Les cures de Napoléon III à Vichy," *ibid.*, XVII (Aug. 15, 1910), 559.

[10] Meredith F. Campbell, *Principles of Urology*, Philadelphia: W. B. Saunders, 1957, pp. 22-23.

[11] R. Scott Stevenson, *Famous Illnesses in History*, London: Eyre & Spottiswoode, 1962, pp. 114-115.

the day the autopsy appeared in print, thought that the autopsy ought to have stated precisely "of what particular disease of both kidneys did Louis Napoleon die." He argued that "atrophy" of one kidney is not necessarily fatal to an elderly man, nor is "sub-acute inflammation of the uriniferous tubes arising from the irritation of a phosphatic calculus in the bladder." On the other hand, he agreed that death had come through the blood as a result of the extensive damage of a vital organ of elimination.[12]

The inadequacy of the autopsy report in this matter was more pointedly criticized the following day by a physician who objected to the initial sentence, namely, that even if it had been suspected that the kidneys were diseased, that "could not have been ascertained." Wrote Dr. Hassall,

> I demur. The impaired constitutional condition of the Emperor, if really attributable to the state of the kidneys, must have been brought about by the impairment of the secretory and excretory functions of the kidneys, matters being retained in the blood which, in a healthy state of these organs, are thrown off and are voided in the urine. The quantity and nature, therefore, of the solid matters contained in such urine, had they been carefully determined beforehand, should, and doubtless would, have revealed the fact that the eliminative powers of the kidneys were impaired, and the conclusion might then have been arrived at with almost absolute certainty that the kidneys were in a diseased condition.[13]

[12] Dr. J. A. Wilson, *Lancet*, I (January 1873), 113-114.

[13] Dr. Arthur Hill Hassall, *Lancet*, I (January 1873), 113.

Since Richard Bright had supplied a description for renal failure in 1827, forty-six years before Napoleon's death, the physicians of 1873 could not have been unaware of the danger of renal failure. In a recent review of the case a British physician notes rather charitably that "it does seem odd that none of them appears at any time to have warned of the likelihood of such an event."[14] Difficult as it is to imagine such neglect in a urinary case, especially one treated by the most eminent men available, we must take seriously Dr. Hassall's inference that the imperial urine had not been satisfactorily analyzed before the operations. The inference deserves our attention not only because the discovery of renal disease at the postmortem examination came as a surprise to the attending physicians, but also because none of the case-reports after Dr. Ferguson's in 1856 reveals explicitly or implicitly that *chemical* tests were made.

Dr. Guillon, for example, when treating the emperor at Biarritz in 1866 for prostatitis, noted sand in the urine and recommended further exploration (which the personal physicians thought to be unnecessary). Evidence does exist, of which more later, that the emperor's urine was occasionally examined in laboratories during the Second Empire, as it was by Dr. Ferguson. But Baron Larrey, Dr. Sée and his committee, and the consultants of 1872-1873 all diagnosed a stone largely on the basis of what they were *told* about symptoms, and it is striking that their descriptions of the emperor's urine tell us what it *looked* like: that it was cloudy, that it contained pus and blood, or that bits of gravel or sand could be found.

[14] Dr. S. F. Marwood, "Louis Napoleon and his Doctors," *Medical Journal of the Southwest*, LXXXII (January 1967), 81.

Though Dr. Sée's report also reveals that he had been told that the urine had contained on occasion "an excess of uric acid and of urates." Moreover, when these various consultations took place, the examiners were asked whether the difficulty was rheumatism and hemorrhoids *or* a stone. Had there been laboratory facilities at the Camp de Châlons, at the Palace of Saint-Cloud, or at Camden Place, perhaps a more thorough examination of the urine would routinely have been done even though the wrong questions might have been asked.

Both Gull and Thompson were sensitive to the criticism, from which we may infer that the results of the autopsy had embarrassed them. Had they suspected that the emperor was on the brink of renal disaster, it is highly unlikely that they would have proceeded with the lithotrity. Gull was the first to offer an excuse. About three months after the emperor's death he told Dr. Debout d'Estrées that he had advised the emperor not to submit to the operation, "the condition of his kidneys being such as to make me fear that any operation would be fatal."[15] What records we have of the pre-operation consultations show, unfortunately for Gull's reputation, that he concurred with the other physicians in the need for an operation. We can only guess at what went on in his mind during the autopsy, but, in the light of his subsequent statement, his departure immediately after it and his refusal to sign the official report tell us that his equivocation began immediately. And Sir Henry Thompson discreetly hinted at precisely that in his notes.[16] Sir Henry was not

[15] Legge, *op. cit.*, p. 87.

[16] Cope, *op. cit.*, p. 63: Gull declined to sign it "for some personal reason, not perhaps difficult to divine."

without guile himself, though his methods were a cut above Sir William's. Thompson simply stuck steadfastly to the statements in the autopsy report, refusing to admit that any mistake had been made. In the eighth edition of his *Clinical Lectures on Diseases of the Urinary Organs*, Thompson revised the twenty-third lecture, in which a case cited bore a striking resemblance to the emperor's, in order to point specifically to the analogy,[17] and then sent proofs of the lecture to many French newspapers.[18]

We must recall that Dr. Sée's case-report was published in several French medical journals at approximately the same time that the autopsy results were published, contributing to an international debate about how long the emperor had suffered from the stone. Without yet being aware of Baron Larrey's diagnosis of 1865, a number of physicians concluded from the size of the stone and from what they now read that the emperor had had this particular stone for at least ten years. Indeed, the accretions that the stone revealed pointed to its development over a period of time and under various circumstances. Just how long, however, was a problem, and a French physician, remembering Dr. Guillon's report published in 1869, believed that ten years was incorrect. Dr. Lapeyrère noted that in 1866 at Vichy Dr. Guillon had passed a probe of tiny caliber without much resistance, enabling the bladder to be emptied. Some gravel had been noted in the urine, but no stone in the bladder.[19] Guillon somewhat

[17] Sir Henry Thompson, *Clinical Lectures on Diseases of the Urinary Organs*, London: Churchill, 8th ed., 1888, p. 305.

[18] Dr. Cabanès, *op. cit.*, II, 432.

[19] Dr. J. Lapeyrère, "A propos de la maladie de Napoléon III," *la France médicale*, XX, #4 (Jan. 15, 1873), 25-28.

later affirmed that Lapeyrère had his facts straight.[20] On the other hand, we know nothing of Guillon's skill, and there is just enough difference between his statements published in 1869 and his interpretations of 1879 to raise legitimate doubt about the thoroughness of his examination in 1866. Moreover, he was obviously a physician who felt that he had been overlooked in Parisian and academic medical circles, saying that his procedures had become standard in coping with urinary problems but that no one attributed them to him.[21] His evident desire to discredit the more eminent physicians who treated Napoleon III after 1866 does nothing to inspire our confidence. What does seem sure is that Napoleon experienced serious urinary difficulties by 1864, and it remains possible that no stone *of any size* had developed by 1866.

In December of 1872 Sir Henry Thompson knew that the stone was of considerable size but he seems not to have considered any other operation than lithotrity as practical. This drew the fire of a number of French doctors. Dr. Lapeyrère simply argued that the age and the general condition of the patient suggested a lithotomy, taking the stone by incision into the bladder rather than crushing it through a series of sessions.[22] This view was echoed by the editors of another French medical journal.[23] Some physicians believed that the decision as to whether to practice lithotomy or lithotrity depended mostly upon the size

[20] Dr. F. Gabriel Guillon, *Oeuvres chirurgicales et médicales du docteur Guillon père*, Paris: Baillière et fils, 1879, p. 225.

[21] *Ibid.*, pp. 11-12.

[22] Lapeyrère, *op. cit.*, p. 28.

[23] "Maladie et mort de Napoléon III," *Lancette française: Gazette des hôpitaux civils et militaires*, XLVI (January 1873), 30-31.

of the stone. Lithotrity, they thought, was suitable only for small calculi. Given the dimensions of the emperor's stone, lithotomy was clearly preferable.[24]

Dr. Guillon believed that success lay in quick operations, no matter what the size of the stone; he practiced a method of lithotrity that limited the patient to two or three sessions of no more than five minutes' duration, the sessions separated by from one to six days depending upon the case. He had been very critical of the more lengthy lithotrity operations which Sir Henry Thompson practiced, saying that they too often ended in death, and he feared that what he called this misuse of lithotrity would revive the use of lithotomy.[25] Guillon's point of view was not so novel as he would have us believe but was essentially that of the pioneer Civiale, whom Thompson had attempted to go beyond. Those French physicians who advocated lithotrity were generally critical of Thompson in every respect in which he differed from Civiale.

Civiale had set down three basic precepts: 1) Always prepare the patient *with care* before beginning the search for and the crushing of the calculus. 2) Wait for the disappearance of all signs of inflammation. 3) Limit the sessions to three or four minutes, and allow an interval of *at least* four days between them. Civiale's disciples thought that Thompson had been violating these basic precepts.[26] Thus, to sum up, the arguments over how to treat the

[24] Dr. Constantin James, *Des causes de la mort de l'empereur*, Paris: Masson, 1873, pp. 3-4.

[25] Dr. Guillon, *op. cit.*, pp. 8-9.

[26] Dr. Rochon (pseud. of Dr. Coorhn), *Des Moyens rationnels de guérison immédiate des retrécissements de l'uètre et de leur complications*, Paris: E. Dentu, 1873, pp. 41-45.

stone fell into three categories: that lithotomy ought to have been used because of the condition of the patient; that lithotomy ought to have been used because of the size of the stone; that Thompson had mishandled the lithotrity. A reading of this particular medical controversy reveals, furthermore, that French medicine felt itself corporately criticized because Napoleon had not been successfully treated before 1870, and that the tendency after 1873 was to dwell upon the shortcomings of British medicine. Few of the French doctors taking part in the controversy considered the matter of uremia, a disease that, as one of them correctly put it, meant that neither lithotrity nor lithotomy would have saved the emperor.[27]

Civiale had taught that chloroform is a dangerous auxiliary in lithotrity,[28] primarily because chloroform can be poisonous to the patient, especially if it has to be used for a series of operations. Also, the patient's sensations help to guide the surgeon's hands in his search for the stone. In Napoleon's case, chloroform was first given during the preliminary examination in December, and again for the two operations. Dr. Edmond Barré and Dr. Constantin James both signed statements criticizing the use of so much chloroform. Barré later insisted that he merely set down Sée's and Ricord's reaction to the operations, but in any case the charge was made that uremia could not have produced such a sudden fatality, and that the emperor's death resulted from chloroform poisoning.[29] A descendant of Dr. Sée, writing in 1939, reflected his ancestor's view

[27] Dr. James, *op. cit.*, p. 27. [28] Dr. Rochon, *op. cit.*, p. 46.

[29] Dr. James, *op. cit.*, pp. 5-6; and Dr. Corvisant, "A propos de la mort de Napoléon III," *la Chronique médicale*, III (July 1, 1896), 413-414.

by saying that the operation would have had a good chance of succeeding had it been done prudently, and particularly if the chloroform had not been given in such heavy doses.[30]

Meanwhile, in 1896, Dr. Cabanès had reviewed the chloroform controversy and had concluded that the charges were groundless. The pathologist who presided at the post-mortem examination had found no evidence of poisoning, and Cabanès correctly noted that Sir Henry Thompson, on the morning after the second operation, had suspected that the emperor's drowsiness revealed renal failure.[31] In other words, he did not die suddenly on December 9, as Dr. James assumed, but had shown the symptoms of the fatal malady two days before death. Moreover, those on the scene immediately after the second operation were satisfied with the patient's progress and showed no alarm.[32] What Cabanès implied was that the charges of improper use of chloroform had come only from the French side of the Channel and from men not present at Camden Place. After Cabanès's investigation, Sir Henry Thompson sent him a letter of thanks for his attempts to keep the record straight.[33]

[30] Dr. E.-Germain Sée, "Un grain de sable dans la vessie d'un empereur," *la Mercure de France*, 292 (June 15, 1939), 598.

[31] Dr. Augustin Cabanès, "La mort de Napoléon III est-elle due au chloroforme?" *la Chronique médicale*, III (June 15, 1896), 355-357.

[32] Baron Corvisart to Eugène Rouher, Jan. 6, 1873, *la Chronique médicale*, III (July 1, 1896), 415-416; and Francis Aubert, *le Gaulois*, Jan. 17, 1873.

[33] Sir Henry Thompson, "Une lettre du Dr. Thompson sur la mort de Napoléon III," *la Chronique médicale*, III (July 15, 1896), 445-446.

Dr. Sée, in his medical lectures after 1873 at the Hôtel-Dieu, often told his students about the consultation of 1870 and always said that he had been the first physician to affirm the presence of the emperor's bladder stone. He accused Nélaton, dead in 1873, so unable to defend himself, of unwillingness to face up to his responsibilities in 1870; Dr. Sée believed to the end that the Empress Eugénie had not known the truth about the emperor's condition.[34] In 1886 Baron Larrey published what he had revealed to Emile Ollivier two years before, namely, that *he* had been the first to diagnose a bladder stone, but had been sworn to secrecy by the emperor.[35]

There the matter rested until 1901, when a Doctor Guépin published a survey of the emperor's case on the twenty-eighth anniversary of his death. Guépin offered no new interpretations, obviously relying on the previous judgment of Dr. Cabanès,[36] but his article provoked others to new speculation. Why, in all the debate, Dr. Gélineau wrote, had no one mentioned the fact that Napoleon III was a diabetic? He had heard this mentioned in professional circles, and it could account for why, even though the lithotrity had been well done, the emperor died so quickly and without great suffering. It would explain the bad state of the kidneys and the blood poisoning, recognized belatedly "by our English colleagues." Dr. Gélineau had also reached the conclusion that the emperor's urine had not been carefully analyzed before the operation, say-

34 Dr. Sécheyron, "La vérité sur la maladie de Napoléon III," *la Chronique médicale*, VIII (March 15, June 15, 1901), 190, 392.

35 *Le Figaro*, February 8, 1886.

36 Dr. A. Guépin, "La maladie, l'opération et la mort de Napoléon III," *la Chronique médicale*, VIII (Jan. 15, 1901), 33-34, 40.

ing that the operation would never have taken place had it been otherwise. With no operation, the emperor would have had to give up walking, riding horseback, and probably even riding in carriages, but he could have lived.[37]

Late in the nineteenth century, the leading French urinary specialist, Dr. Félix Guyon, had been teaching that diabetes is often associated with other urinary difficulties, especially in cases where stricture of the urethra is found.[38] Consequently, Dr. Gélineau may have been reflecting latter-day speculation about the emperor's case in the light of the new teaching. Dr. Guépin responded that the new argument was mere speculation, that no evidence existed to support Gélineau's hypothesis that Napoleon III had been a diabetic: he had died from infection and from uric poisoning.[39] In response to that, a doctor in Orléans entered the fray to say that such evidence did exist. He said that a pharmacist in Orléans, M.-G. Renault, had interned in Parisian hospitals and had worked regularly in the laboratory formerly operated by Professor Mialhe, a pharmacist to the emperor. On various occasions Mialhe had been given samples of the imperial urine by Dr. Corvisart for analysis. Renault said that particularly during the years 1866-1868 the urine was very cloudy, very ammoniac, but that "it contained no more sugar. I say contained *no more*, because the chemist had

[37] Dr. Gélineau, "La mort de Napoléon III," *la Chronique médicale*, VIII (February 15, 1901), 127-128.

[38] Dr. J.-C.-Félix Guyon, *Leçons cliniques sur les maladies des voies urinaires professées à l'Hôpital Necker*, Paris: Baillière et fils, 1894-1897, *passim*.

[39] Dr. A. Guépin, "A propos de la mort de Napoléon III," *la Chronique médicale*, VIII (March 1, 1901), 154-157.

come to the conclusion that at that time the urine had to be diabetic."[40] The last word on the subject came from Dr. Witkowski and was really a conventional defense of the physicians of 1873. He found it inconceivable that they could have been slipshod when it came to a preliminary examination of the urine, nor could he accept the statement that Dr. Thompson and company had not considered the possibility of diabetes or kidney disease.[41] But he had no new facts, merely a great faith in medical infallibility.

At this late date, the medical case of Napoleon III must remain a matter of historical probability. Nevertheless, some of the mysteries seem less mysterious in the light of contemporary medicine, and a century of medical debate on the case has left valuable evidence susceptible of modern analysis. The emperor's death, first of all, resulted from kidney failure, uremic poisoning, and septicemic shock, rather than from the bladder stone itself. No doubt the operations to crush the stone hastened the renal failure. The repeated rigors experienced by the emperor revealed the pain and shock, and probably the spread of infection. Had the true state of his kidneys been suspected, it seems unlikely that Sir Henry Thompson would have attempted the lithotrity.

Whether the bladder stone partly crushed in 1873 was the original calculus cannot be ascertained. Its unusual size might suggest longevity, but the chemical composition of its outer layers points to a fast-growing calculus.

[40] Dr. Fauchon, "Toujours à propos de la mort de Napoléon III," *la Chronique médicale*, VIII (March 15, 1901), 191.

[41] Dr. Gustave Witkowski, *Comment moururent les rois de France*, Paris: Bibliothèque des Curieux, 1920, pp. 192-193.

More than one stone could have formed during the 1860's, to be painfully expelled in the urine. Several of the emperor's related ailments strongly suggest lithemia and force us to presume that the painful crises of 1865, 1866, and 1869 all involved gravel or stones, cystitis, and pyelonephritis. The evidence also suggests some degree of prostatism, which would have complicated the symptoms for Napoleon's diagnosticians. The urethral strictures that were treated on several occasions, though suggesting the possibility of calculi, were insufficient proof of their presence. Such strictures may be produced by other infections or traumas.

Bladder calculi are common and may originate in a variety of ways. The fact that no stones were found in the kidneys at the time of the autopsy indicates that the emperor's vesical calculus had not originated there. In his case, since there was evidence of gout, and since the nucleus of the stone was composed of uric acid and urates, we must surmise that the emperor's calculus was originally a complication of gout. The growth of the stone, with its phosphatic layers, may well have mirrored the mineralized waters imbibed at Vichy, but this particular type of layer also implies some degree of vesical infection and probably some obstruction of the neck of the bladder, which would have been extremely painful.

The very existence of related maladies illustrates the difficulty in diagnosing the emperor's diseases precisely. Several of the physicians assured the emperor that he did not have a stone, because his symptoms were merely those of rheumatism or gout, but they should have known that the tendency to gout may well mean a tendency to stones. That uric acid in the blood is the specific cause of gouty deposits was known after 1848, just as it was known that the condition, if not checked, could lead to the formation of uric acid stones.[42] The hypersensitivity of the emperor's cutaneous nerves, for example, described at the time of Dr. Ferguson's examination in 1856, might be called neuralgia today. Since we know that he suffered from rheumatism and gout, meaning that we may call him an arthritic, one possibility is that his neuralgia was related to arthritis. On the other hand, this cutaneous and muscular hypersensitivity could have been his body's response to the inflammation of gout, which is a generalized disease even though it manifests itself more spectacularly in specific sites such as the left great toe. All the evidence in the case points to gout nephropathy. Gout is not generally included among the many forms of rheumatic or arthritic disease, because it is caused by a disorder of protein metabolism. Yet it is a disease that causes damage to the joints. Uric acid is deposited in the cartilage that covers the joint surfaces.

The earliest of the arthritic symptoms appeared during Louis-Napoleon's imprisonment at Ham, where he also first developed hemorrhoids. Inactivity, a change in diet, and prolonged sitting on cold surfaces all could contribute to hemorrhoids, and they may also be produced psychosomatically.[43] As the months of confinement in that dank fortress lengthened into years, the prisoner's depression and recurring headaches were noted by his

[42] Dr. W.S.C. Copeman, *A Short History of the Gout and the Rheumatic Diseases*, Berkeley and Los Angeles: University of California Press, 1964, pp. 106-107; and *Lancet*, 1 (January 1873), 59.

[43] Dr. A.T.W. Simeons, *Man's Presumptuous Brain*, New York: E. P. Dutton, 1962, p. 141.

visitors. While hemorrhoids are not primarily caused by depression and tension, those conditions can cause constipation, and hemorrhoids may be the result. Prisons like Ham still exist in the world today, and the prisoners in them, even if they are properly fed and treated, almost always show signs of physical deterioration. Especially they display peripheral vascular problems like varicosities in the extremities, hemorrhoids, or inflammatory conditions of the joints, all of which usually persist for the duration of an individual's life. The depression and anxiety of Ham reappeared in the emperor in 1855, and the first reports of attacks of gout came soon after, some months before Dr. Ferguson was summoned.

Thomas Sydenham, in the seventeenth century, was the first to suggest a relationship between gout and intellectual ability. That association was noted again in 1927 by Havelock Ellis: "Genius is not a product of gout, but it may be that the gouty poison acts as a real stimulus to intellectual ability and a real aid to intellectual achievement."[44] These time-honored suspicions have been given scientific sanction by studies which show that significant levels of uric acid (and perhaps other purines like caffeine and theobromine) stimulate the cerebral cortex. Serum uric acid levels, in other words, are highly correlated with the personal characteristics of drive, achievement, and leadership: as two investigators have put it, "a tendency to gout is a tendency to the executive suite."[45] With all due respect to Queen Hortense's efforts to imbue

[44] Copeman, *op. cit.*, p. 82.

[45] George W. Brooks and Ernst Mueller, "Serum Urate Concentrations Among University Professors," *Journal of the American Medical Association*, cvc (Feb. 7, 1966), 415-418.

her son with a sense of his Napoleonic duty, we must confess that his notable devotion to that cause was abetted by his bodily chemistry.

What is more, people with high serum uric acid do not feel driven but find their tasks and responsibilities to be pleasant and not unduly burdensome—in contrast to people high in cholesterol, who tend to feel overburdened. We would have to assume that anyone with Napoleon III's responsibilities during the Crimean War would inevitably have experienced many anxieties, but the cumulative evidence, political and medical, reveals no hint of regret that he had assumed what Louis XIV called *le métier de roi*. The depression the emperor exhibited after 1855, in other words, had its roots in something deeper than the daily exigencies of his office.

Could His Majesty have been a diabetic, as was proposed in 1901? Here the evidence is skimpy, for none of his physicians seems to have suspected that particular malady. Some evidence does exist, of course, and furthermore there are many interesting analogies between gout and diabetes as metabolic disorders, even though gout manifests itself in the skeleton. The tendency to both diseases is inherited, and both have "fat-type" and "lean-type" manifestations. The form of diabetes associated with obesity (the stable form) comes on later in life, is generally produced by emotional stress, is associated with an increase in body-weight, and is not characterized by comas or by retinal changes in the eye.[46] In the absence of more concrete or convincing evidence, we can do little more than note that the depression and frustration Napoleon III began to suffer early in his reign *could* have instigated

[46] Simeons, *op. cit.*, pp. 204-220.

a mild case of diabetes as well as his attacks of gout. The "fat-type" of subject, as the emperor increasingly was, is fortunate in suffering less severe attacks of gout than do the "lean-types." But it has been discovered that the overweight gout patient in particular usually has some deep-seated emotional problem which he is notably skillful in concealing behind a placid facial expression.[47] Such a physiognomy squares well with Napoleon's reputation as the sphinx of the Tuileries.

The symptoms which Dr. Ferguson diagnosed as "nervous exhaustion" in 1856 he thought were produced by overwork and lack of exercise, and he feared that the emperor might be well on the road to epilepsy. The expression "nervous exhaustion" became neurasthenia later in the nineteenth century and was used to describe a state of emotional or nervous exhaustion that left a person weak, fatigued, listless, depressed, and without zest. In particular, neurasthenia implied a debilitating impact upon sexual appetite and performance. Today, neurasthenia would be classified as a neurosis produced by emotional conflict, characterized not merely by the fatigue and depression Dr. Ferguson reported but by fears and phobias as well. The attacks of anxiety which Napoleon III experienced on several occasions at night are not at all unusual in neurasthenia: acute anxiety or panic reactions. The subject will have great difficulty in mobilizing his energies, and he will often be impotent. Men under fifty, as Napoleon III was at the time, rarely suffer from impotence for physical reasons; one of the chief psychological reasons is a frigid wife with whom sexual relations are

[47] *Ibid.*, pp. 236-241.

unsatisfactory.[48] We know already that the emperor's disappointment in his marriage preceded the onset of this neurasthenia and that he confessed to Dr. Ferguson not merely the decline in sexual activity but its lack of satisfaction, obviously something quite new to him. In those days, increased sexual activity was thought to lead to exhaustion or impotence, but that notion has statistically been proven to be wrong. Sexual inactivity leads to impotence; and fears, worries, or anxieties lead to the inactivity.[49]

The array of Napoleon's ailments compels our sympathy as it becomes evident that he was rarely free of pain during most of his reign. It also becomes clear why his contemporaries, aware of his recurring distress, baffled by his methods of governance, astounded by the disasters which followed closely upon his triumphs, fell upon his illnesses as accountable for mysteries otherwise inexplicable. Moreover, an individual under the influence of an illness or a disease will seem to be altered, so that it is easy to assume that controversial or incorrect decisions have been the effect of disease. We all know of individuals whose behavior and judgment are deeply affected by ailments of even minor medical significance; history also knows of individuals, like Cardinal Richelieu for example, who suffered constantly, yet were not deflected from their courses nor displayed any flagging of their wills. The character of the afflicted individual, in other words,

[48] Dr. Samuel H. Kraines, *The Therapy of the Neuroses and Psychoses*, Philadelphia: Lea & Febiger, 1948, pp. 32, 110, 116.

[49] Simeons, *op. cit.*, p. 245.

determines to a significant degree the effect disease has upon him.

The neurasthenia aside for a moment, the medical record of Napoleon fails entirely to provide substantial proof for a single example of a political decision that would have been made differently had the emperor been free of arthritis, gout, hemorrhoids, or the stone. Mistakes were made and policies went sour, but through it all and even after defeat we see his unswerving faith in the cause he represented, a gentle obstinacy. The decisions for peace in 1866 and for war in 1870 may remain forever controversial as to their wisdom, but neither was made hastily *nor by the emperor alone.* Good health would have been no guarantee of freedom from error, given the particular factors that determined those particular decisions.

On the other hand, the incompatibility of the imperial marriage did to an important degree affect the politics of the Second Empire. The emperor overcame the attacks of neurasthenia which threatened his stability in 1856 and learned to live with his marital disappointment, though we can hardly say that his subsequent amorous escapades were a satisfying substitute for the domestic bliss he had envisioned. From their alienation, however, grew the empress's determination to steer an independent political course. Though she had little to do with the formation of policies, she spoke about them freely, independently, and in ways that jeopardized their integrity. Without question she inadvertently misled the Austrians during the eighteen-sixties as to the emperor's real intentions and his capacity to govern. In 1870, as regent, she was only too willing to turn out the new liberal government whose prestige had been one of the major determinants in the decision to declare war, and her appraisal of the national crisis after the initial defeats prevented the retreat upon Paris that Napoleon and MacMahon preferred and led straight to Sedan.

The intellectuals of the Second Empire, almost to the last man, were contemptuous of Napoleon III, believing him to be unspeakably mediocre. No one put that contempt more plainly than did Charles Baudelaire when he wrote that "Napoleon III's great claim to renown will have been that he showed how anybody at all, if only he gets hold of the telegraph and the printing-presses, can govern a great nation . . . and fame is the result of the matching of a personality with the national stupidity."[50] Such hostility haunted the memory of the emperor for many decades after 1873, and only now, as we approach the centennial of his death, is it apparent that the passions have been withering and that a new Napoleon III has been emerging for some years. In his last will and testament, dated April 24, 1865,[51] the emperor recommended that his son undertake a serious study of the acts and the writings of the "prisoner of St. Helena," but added advice that would not have come from St. Helena: "Power is a heavy burden. You cannot always do the good you would like to do, and your contemporaries are seldom fair. A man, therefore, must do his work and have faith in himself, a sense of his duty." The words for the son well serve the father.

[50] Charles Baudelaire, *The Essence of Laughter and Other Essays, Journals, and Letters*, ed. by Peter Quennell, New York: Meridian, 1956, p. 186.

[51] Suzanne Desternes and Henriette Chandet, *Louis Prince Impérial, 1856-1879*, Paris: Hachette, 1957, p. 122; and Octave Aubry, *The Second Empire*, New York: Lippincott, 1940, pp. 302-303.

Bibliography

This bibliography, divided into six sections, is not intended to be a general bibliography of works on either Napoleon III or the Second Empire. Rather, the sections are designed to serve readers who have specialized interests in the Second Empire and to offer them commentaries on sources that are either obscure or controversial. Political monographs cited in full in the footnotes are not included in the bibliography.

ARCHIVAL SOURCES

Archives du Musée du Val-de-Grâce:

Carton 109: Biographical notes on Baron Hippolyte Larrey.

Carton 113: Baron Larrey's duties at the Camp de Châlons.
Cartons 118-119: Dispatches from military doctors in 1870-1871.
Carton 202: "Souvenirs du Baron Larrey," collected by M. Carette.

[The Larrey will left various items and papers to several institutions in Paris and were distributed by his heir, Mlle. Juliette Dodu. When a young girl whose mother managed the post office in Pithiviers, she was a heroine of the Franco-Prussian War. Juliette intercepted enemy dispatches for the French forces until she was detected and sentenced to be shot. Her life was spared by the crown prince.]

Carton 207³: #754 on Dr. Guillon.
Carton 209/I: dossier 991, biographical notes on Dr. Lévy.

Bibliothèque Nationale; Département des Manuscrits: Nouvelles Acquisitions Françaises:

#5887-5892: Correspondence of Baron Hippolyte Larrey.

[#5887 contains letters from foreign doctors to Dr. Larrey. #5888-5890 contain Larrey's letters through the Second Empire and provide much information on the medical world. Students of Flaubert will find a letter from Larrey to Flaubert (1868) on the effects of absinthe in #5889.]

#1066-1067: Letters of Napoleon III to Mme. Cornu.

[In his own difficult hand. The absence of letters between 1852 and 1860 reflects her hostility to his dictatorship. After 1873 a few letters from Blanchard Jerrold to Mme. Cornu are included in the collection.]

Archives Nationales:

O⁵ 80: Members of the imperial household.
O⁵ 98: A dossier of personnel.
O⁵ 120: The dossier of Dr. Conneau.
F¹⁷ 3578: Dr. Gabriel Andral.
F¹⁷ 3579: Dr. Jean Bouillaud.
F¹⁷ 3580: Dr. Baron Jules Cloquet.
F¹⁷ 3683: Dr. Henri Conneau.

F^{17} 3684: Dr. Antoine-Sulpice Fauvel, Dr. Baron Hippolyte Larrey, Dr. Auguste Nélaton.

F^{17} 3685: Dr. Germain Sée.

Cartons C.1338 (210) and C.1339 (191): Dr. Henri Conneau.

Archives de la Préfecture de Police:

B a/957: Dossier of Marguerite Bellanger.

E a/22 6: Dossier of Symphorien-C. Boitelle. Prefect of police after the Orsini attempt, in office from March 16, 1858, to February 21, 1866, when he became a senator.

B a/1002: Dossier of Virginia de Verazi, Countess of Castiglione.

E a/113: Dossier of Jacques-François Griscelli de Vezzani, called Arthur or Baron de Rimini.

B a/1.138: Dossier of Michel Lagrange. A commissaire de police and chef du service politique. Present at Chislehurst to protect Napoleon III from refugees of the Commune.

B a/1.017: Dossier of Dr. Henri Conneau.

B a/1.019: Dossier of Dr. Baron Lucien Corvisart.

E a/89 and B a/1165: Dossiers of Gustave Macé. Chef de la sûreté 1879-1884, the successor to M. Claude, a police reformer who was often balked by higher authority.

B a/120 4: Dossier of A.-E.-O., Comte de Nieuwerkerque.

E a/22 7: Dossier of Joachim-Marie Piétri. Prefect of police after Boitelle in 1866.

E a/22 5: Dossier of Pierre-Marie Piétri. Prefect of police who resigned after the Orsini attempt in 1858, later an administrator for the Comté de Nice.

PAPERS FOUND IN THE TUILERIES, 1870
(Editions in the Bibliothèque Nationale)

Footnotes to these papers in works on the Second Empire are usually truncated and misleading. Furthermore, various editions exclude critical documents. The first example cited seems to be the most inclusive of the various choices and is the only edition to include Dr. Sée's case-report of July 3, 1870, found in the papers of Dr. Henri Conneau. The call numbers are those of the Bibliothèque Nationale.

Lb^{56}. 472: *Papiers et correspondance de la famille impériale*, 2 vols., Paris: Imprimerie Nationale, 1870-1872. There were three later editions of this title.

Lb^{56}. 474: *Documents authentiques annotés. Les papiers secrets du Second Empire*, Brussels: Office de Publicité, 1870-1871.

Lb^{56}. 476: *Papiers sauvés des Tuileries*, ed. by Robert Halt, Paris: E. Dentu, 1871.

Lb^{56}. 477: *Papiers secrets et correspondance du Second Empire. Réimpression complète* . . . par A. Poulet-Malassis, France and Belgium: 1871. This title ran to at least eight editions.

Lb^{56}. 478: *Les Papiers secrets des Tuileries* (Le Dossier du Nord), Lille, 1871. A brief volume including papers concerned solely with le Nord.

Lb^{56}. 479: *Papiers secrets brûlés dans l'incendie des Tuileries*, Brussels: Rosez, 1871.

Lb^{56}. 480: *Les petits Papiers secrets des Tuileries et de Saint-Cloud étiquetés par un collectionneur*, Vol. I, Paris: E. Dentu, 1871; Vol. II, Brussels: chez Vanderauwera, 1871.

MEMOIRS AND LETTERS

Ambès, Baron d' (pseud. of Georges-Charles d'Anthès, Baron Heeckeren), *Mémoires inédits sur Napoléon III*, Paris: Société des publications littéraires illustrées, 1909; or *Intimate Memoirs of Napoleon III*, 2 vols., London: St. Paul, 1912. An early supporter of Louis-Napoleon who sat in the Senate from 1852 to 1870. His recollections are quite unreliable.

Aubert, Francis, *Le Journal de Chislehurst, du 9 au 17 janvier 1873*, Paris: E. Lachaud, 1873. Aubert arrived at Chislehurst a few moments before Napoleon's death. This report of that death and the funeral was sent to *le Gaulois*.

Barthez de Marmorières, Dr. Ernest, *The Empress Eugénie and Her Circle*, London: T. Fisher Unwin, 1912; and *La*

Famille impériale à Saint-Cloud et à Biarritz, Paris: Calmann-Lévy, 1913. Both books are largely letters written by Barthez, a shrewd and kindly observer, to his wife between 1856 and 1865.

Bavoux, Evariste, *Chislehurst. Tuileries, souvenirs intimes sur l'Empereur*, Paris: E. Dentu, 1873. Bavoux was a former conseiller de l'Empire, a conservative Bonapartist who regretted the political reforms of the 1860's.

Beust, Friedrich Ferdinand, Graf von, *Memoirs*, 2 vols., London: Remington, 1887; and *Le Dernier des Napoléon*, Paris: Lacroix, Verboeckoven, 1872. Beust was a Saxon minister who passed into Austrian service after 1866. The latter title is a good example of the polemical literature published after 1870 and reveals more about Beust than about Napoleon III.

Beyens, Baron Napoléon-Eugène-Louis-Joseph-Marie-Auguste, *Le Second Empire vu par un diplomate belge*, 2 vols., Paris: Plon-Nourrit, 1924-1926. The author is actually the son of the Belgian minister to Paris, who began his career there in 1853 as a secretary, dying there in 1894 as minister plenipotentiary. The book relies heavily on the father's papers as well as upon the son's recollections, and reveals the eternal Belgian fear of French expansion.

Bicknell, Anna L., *Life in the Tuileries under the Second Empire*, London: T. Fisher Unwin, 1895. She lived in the Tuileries for nine years, ca. 1857 to 1866, as governess for the daughters of Comte (later Duc) Charles de Tascher de la Pagerie, the Beauharnais cousin who served as grand maître to the empress.

Blanc, Louis, *Histoire de dix ans, 1830-1840*, 5 vols., Paris: Pagnerre, 1841-1844. Volume v gives a brief account of the Strasbourg fiasco of 1836. Blanc had visited Louis-Napoleon at Ham and had a more favorable view of him than he would in his later *1848, Historical Revelations*, London: Chapman & Hall, 1858, where he tells of his visit to Ham.

Bonaparte, Princesse Mathilde, "Souvenirs des années d'exil,"

Revue des deux mondes, XLII (Dec. 15, 1927), 721-752, and XLIII (Jan. 1, 1928), 76-105. Princess Mathilde began work on her memoirs toward the end of the Second Empire at the suggestion of Sainte-Beuve. After the war, she continued work, intending to dedicate the memoirs to Claudius Popelin, the successor to Comte Nieuwerkerque in her affections, but ceased work when the liaison ended. These articles were extracts from her manuscript published by her nephew and heir, Count Primoli, whose own death halted further publications.

Carette, Mme. (Mlle. Bouvet), *Recollections of the Court of the Tuileries*, New York: D. Appleton, 1890. Useful observations by a woman in the empress's circle.

Castelnau, General Henri, "Sedan et Wilhelmshöhe" (Journal du Général Castelnau, aide-de-camp de Napoléon III), ed. by Louis Sonolet, *la Revue de Paris*, XXXVI (Oct. 1, 1929), 499-521; (Oct. 15, 1929), 851-874; (Nov. 1, 1929), 167-203. The three installments cover July 28, 1870, to March 20, 1871, and are useful for dating decisions on the campaign and the events of the emperor's imprisonment.

Chevalier, Michel, "Journal de Michel Chevalier (1865-1869)," *Revue des deux mondes*, ed. by Marcel Blanchard, series 8, XII (Nov. 1, 1932), 173-189. Chevalier, the well-known Saint-Simonian, became a senator in 1865. The journal comprised part of Chevalier's papers in the possession of his granddaughter, Mlle. Flourens.

Cornu, Mme. Hortense, "Louis-Napoleon Painted by a Contemporary," *Cornhill Magazine*, XXVII (Jan.-June, 1873), 595-614. This article was derived shortly after the emperor's death from four different earlier conversations N. W. Senior had with Mme. Cornu. She is one of the best sources on Napoleon's character.

Cowley, H.R.C.W., First Earl, *The Paris Embassy during the Second Empire*, ed. by F. A. Wellesley (his son), London: T. Butterworth, 1928. The American edition was entitled *Secrets of the Second Empire*, New York: Harper & Bros., 1929. Cowley was British Ambassador to Paris in 1852-1867 and a superior observer of the imperial scene. The book is derived from the Cowley Papers in the Public Record Office (F. O. 519). A second volume derived from these papers is Sir Victor Wellesley and Robert Sencourt, *Conversations with Napoleon III*, London: E. Benn, 1934; it has the additional advantage of the use of documents in Vienna, especially Metternich's papers, which had the effect of undermining the Oncken thesis.

Duruy, Victor, *Notes et Souvenirs*, 2 vols., Paris: Hachette, 1901. Duruy was the liberal minister of public instruction from 1863 to 1869. His second volume contains a chapter on Napoleon III.

Ernest II, Duke of Saxe-Coburg-Gotha, *Memoirs*, 4 vols., London: Remington, 1888-1890. The last two volumes cover the period of the Second Empire. While Ernest has some favorable things to say about Napoleon III and was one of the first monarchs to accept him, he showed increasing suspicions after 1859, thus reflecting the belief of his brother (Prince Albert) that Napoleon was essentially militant and might seize the leadership of the German national movement after the success in Italy.

[Eugénie] Alba, Duke of, ed., *Lettres familières de l'Impératrice Eugénie*, 2 vols., Paris: Le Divan, 1935. Especially valuable for depicting the empress's disenchantment with power and her marriage. Also see Maurice Paléologue, *The Tragic Empress: Conversations of the Empress Eugénie, 1901-1919*, New York and London: Harper & Bros., 1928. Dated memories, of course, but they do the empress honor. If they must be used with care, they still must be used.

[Evans] Crane, Dr. Edward A., ed., *The Memoirs of Dr. Thomas W. Evans: The Second French Empire*, New York: D. Appleton, 1905. Crane was one of the executors of Evans' will. The volume contains only those parts of Evans' writing that covered the Second Empire when he was the imperial dentist.

Faucher, Léon-L.-J., *Vie parlementaire*, Paris: Amyot, 1867. This is actually the second volume of his publication, the first volume being correspondence. Faucher's recollections are especially important for the Second Republic when he was briefly minister of the interior.

Filon, Augustin, *Memoirs of the Prince Imperial (1856-1879)*, London: W. Heinemann, 1913; and *Recollections of the Empress Eugénie*, London and New York: Cassell, 1920. Filon, a teacher, was chosen by Victor Duruy in 1867 to be in charge of the prince imperial's education, a post he kept until 1875 even though the prince went to a formal school, Woolwich Royal Academy, beginning in the fall of 1872. The empress allowed him to use the prince's correspondence, and he had the collaboration of her secretary, Franceschini Piétri. His recollections of the empress were not to be published until her death, which occurred on July 11, 1920, Filon having died in 1916.

Fleury, General Comte E.-Félix, *Souvenirs*, 2 vols., Paris: Plon-Nourrit, 1897-1898. Fleury was perhaps one of the best friends Napoleon III had, and had a higher opinion of the emperor's military skills than did most other generals. His recollections of the Italian campaign are particularly useful.

Fraser, Sir William Augustus, Bart., *Napoleon III (My Recollections)*, London: Sampson, Low, Marston, 1896. Interesting observations over a period of years by a man widely acquainted in British politics and an M.P. He had a high opinion of the emperor's character.

Granier de Cassagnac, B.-Adolphe, *Souvenirs du Second Empire*, 3 vols., Paris: E. Dentu, 1879-1882. A Bonapartist polemicist both before and after 1870, and the father of Paul de Cassagnac who was captured at Sedan. The chapter on Sedan in Vol. III is especially significant as it was seen and corrected by Napoleon III.

Halévy, Ludovic, *Carnets*, 2 vols., Paris: Calmann-Lévy, 1935. A friend of Morny who thought his loss in 1865 was irreparable for the empire, Halévy was a man of real intelligence and too sophisticated to be easily classified.

Heeckeren, Baron; see Ambès.

[Hortense], *Mémoires de la Reine Hortense*, 3 vols., published by Prince Napoleon with notes by Jean Hanoteau, Paris: Librairie Plon, 1927. Useful for the childhood of Napoleon III.

Hübner, Alexander von, *Neuf ans de souvenirs d'un ambassadeur d'Autriche à Paris, 1851-1859* (Joseph de Hübner), 2 vols., Paris: Plon, 1904. Hübner was inferior to Cowley as a foreign observer of the imperial scene.

Jarras, General Hugues-Louis, *Souvenirs*, Paris: Plon, 1892. He served primarily under Bazaine during the Franco-Prussian War.

La Chapelle, Alfred Comte de, *Œuvres posthumes et autographes inédits de Napoléon III en exil*, Paris: E. Lachaud, 1873. Despite the title, most of the writing was by La Chapelle, but much of what he wrote was suggested and seen by the emperor. La Chapelle was a loyal courtier at Camden Place.

Lanusse, L'abbé Eugène, *Sedan, l'heure suprême*, Paris: Flammarion, 1892. While Lanusse was an eyewitness at Sedan, the greater significance of his book is as a piece of post-1871 patriotic literature to prove, among other things, the patriotism of a priest.

Lebrun, General B.-L.-Joseph, *Souvenirs militaires, 1866-1870*, Paris: E. Dentu, 1895; and *Bazeilles-Sedan*, Paris: E. Dentu, 1891. Lebrun was an aide to Napoleon III at the outbreak of the Franco-Prussian War, but when the emperor relinquished supreme command Lebrun was put in charge of the XII Corps, part of the new army being formed at the Camp de Châlons.

Macé, Gustave, *La Police parisienne. Le Service de la sûreté*, Paris: Charpentier, 1884. While Macé's headship of the Sûreté came after the Second Empire, he had the use of M. Claude's private papers. The published memoirs of M. Claude are spurious. (See last section.)

Malmesbury, James Howard Harris, third Earl of, *Memoirs of an Ex-Minister*, 2 vols., London: Longmans, Green, 1884-1885. He knew Louis-Napoleon for many years, though not so long or so perceptively as Hortense Lacroix Cornu did.

Meding, Oskar, *De Sadowa à Sedan: Mémoires d'un ambassadeur secret aux Tuileries*, ed. by Victor Tissot, Paris: E. Dentu, 1885. Meding was Prussian-born, but took service in the government of George V of Hanover, a legitimist who detested the Bonapartes. In 1860, however, Napoleon III won the king's gratitude by decorating him. Meding followed his king into exile after the defeat of 1866 and was then sent to Paris as a secret ambassador to work for the restoration of George V by fomenting war between France and Prussia.

Mels, A. (pseud. of Martin Cohn), *Wilhelmshoehe, souvenirs de la captivité de Napoléon III*, Paris: A. Dupont, 1880. A German journalist who had long been aware of Napoleon III's sympathies for Germany. He was hired by the London *Times* to interview the emperor in prison.

Ménière, Dr. Prosper, *Mémoires anecdotiques sur les salons du Second Empire. Journal du Dr. Prosper Ménière, publié par son fils, le Dr. E. Ménière*, Paris: Plon-Nourrit, 1903. Many anecdotes, but no useful medical information about the emperor.

Mercy-Argenteau, Comtesse Louise de (née Princesse de Caraman-Chimay), *The Last Love of an Emperor*, London: Iris, 1916. The memoirs were written during 1875 and 1876, but were not published while her husband was alive. She died in 1890, after which her heir refrained from publishing the manuscript because of many things in it offensive to Bismarck and Germany. The book is important if not entirely reliable.

Mérimée, Prosper, *Correspondance générale*, 16 vols., Paris: Le Divan, 1941-1961. Volumes XIII-XV cover the years 1866-1870. Mérimée was a longtime friend of the Montijo family and thus a court figure of the Second Empire. He had a highly pessimistic view of people and events, and was no friend of the liberalizing of the empire.

[Metternich] Salomon, Henry, *L'Ambassade de Richard de*

Metternich à Paris, Paris: Firmin-Didot, 1931. A useful book heavily based on the Metternich correspondence. That correspondence is also utilized in Count E. C. Corti, "Les Idées de l'impératrice Eugénie sur le redressement de la carte de l'Europe, d'après des rapports du prince Richard de Metternich," *Revue des études napoléoniennes*, XIX (July-Dec., 1922), 147-155; and in Corti, "L'Empereur Napoléon III après Sadowa (1886)," *ibid.*, 221-228.

Metternich-Winneburg, Pauline C.M.W., *Souvenirs de la princesse de Metternich, 1859-1871*, Paris: Plon-Nourrit, 1922. Princess Pauline was devoted to the imperial couple. Her memoirs mostly portray high society.

Monts, General Graf Karl von, *La Captivité de Napoléon en Allemagne*, Paris: Pierre Lafitte, 1910. Monts was the governor of Cassel and had the responsibility for Napoleon III at Wilhelmshöhe. His work was heavily used by Paul Guériot and Henri Welschinger.

Moskowa, General Prince de la, "Quelques notes intimes sur la guerre de 1870," *le Correspondant*, Dec. 10, 1898, pp. 957-971. An eyewitness account of Sedan by one of Napoleon's aides-de-camp.

[Moulton, Mme. Charles, née Lillie Greenough] Laurière, Y.-H. de, *Une Américaine à la cour de Napoléon III*, Paris: Calmann-Lévy, 1938. Mrs. Moulton was a prominent singer. She left memoirs entitled *In the Courts of Memory 1858-1875*, London: Harper, 1912.

[Napoleon III] Corti, Count E. C., "Correspondance du roi Louis et de Louis-Napoléon interceptée par la police de Metternich, 1833-1840: (Première partie) Louis-Napoléon et son projet de mariage avec la princesse Mathilde"; (deuxième partie) "Les Complots de Louis-Napoléon et l'état d'ame de son père," *Revue des études napoléoniennes*, XXVI (Jan.-June 1926), 156-176, 233-250.

Ollivier, Emile, *Lettres de l'exil, 1870-1874*, Paris: Hachette, 1921. The defeated and embittered Ollivier. His true devotion to Napoleon III is revealed in these letters.

Paget, Sir James, *Memoirs and Letters*, London and New

York: Longmans, Green, 1901. Unfortunately, he is discreet about the diagnosis of Napoleon's disorders.

Pajol, General Comte Charles-Pierre-Victor, *Lettre de M. le général Pajol sur la capitulation de Sedan*, Paris: Lefebvre, 1871. (Reprinted from the *Moniteur universel*, July 22, 1871.) Pajol was with the emperor at Sedan and wrote his open letter to justify the emperor's conduct at the time the National Assembly was beginning a formal inquiry into the Government of National Defense and the Commune of 1871.

[Pujol], "Journal de l'abbé Pujol," *Revue des deux mondes*, LII (July 15, 1929), 299-319. Pujol became chaplain at the Tuileries in 1869. His journal provides good information about the empress, especially between July 31 and August 6, 1870.

Randon, Comte, J.-L.-C.-A., *Mémoires du maréchal Randon*, 2 vols., Paris: Typographie Lahure, 1875-1877. In Vol. II there is a long description of his views in 1866 when he was the champion of a military demonstration along the Rhine.

Schneider, Commandant, *Le Second Empire à Saint-Cloud*, Paris: Victor-Havard, 1894. Schneider had been a palace steward who published some of his material anonymously in *le Figaro*, July 28, 1883. In his book he complained bitterly about having been plagiarized by Mme. Carette in her 1890 publication.

Senior, Nassau William, *Conversations with Distinguished Persons during the Second Empire from 1860-1863*, 2 vols., London: Hurst & Blackett, 1880. On the face of it, Senior's volumes ought to be of great value. Too much of the information, however, suffers from obvious partisanship and contemporaneity. Eminent people do not necessarily seem to be well informed, and much of their concern is for the future—in other words, speculation. Only when we come across a witness like Mme. Cornu, who knew the subject of her testimony intimately for a long time, does the material really become valuable.

Tascher de la Pagerie, Comtesse Stéphanie de, *Mon Séjour aux Tuileries, 1852-1871*, Paris: Paul Ollendorff, 1893. The three volumes cover: I (1852-1858); II (1859-1865); III (1866-1871). As a Beauharnais relative by marriage, she was discreet, favorable to the dynasty, and a courtier.

Tocqueville, Alexis de, *Recollections*, New York: Meridian Books, 1959. Part III concerns the formation of Louis-Napoleon's government in 1848, in which Tocqueville had the foreign ministry. He began writing the third part in 1851; thus it is a contemporary observation of Louis-Napoleon written in the immediate aftermath of Tocqueville's estrangement.

Vandam, Albert Dresden, *An Englishman in Paris*, 2 vols., New York: D. Appleton, n.d.; and *Undercurrents of the Second Empire*, New York: G. P. Putnam's Sons, 1896. These are gossipy books written long after the events described, by a man who kept no journal. He often implied a contemporary observation that could only have been hindsight. Moreover, he must be used cautiously, as he was a malicious busybody and a snob.

Verly, Baron Albert, *Souvenirs du Second Empire: les étapes douloureuses (l'empereur, de Metz à Sedan)*, Paris: Daragon, 1908. This Verly was the son of Colonel Baron Jacques-Albert Verly who commanded the Cent-Gardes. The book is based on letters written home by the Colonel during the campaign of 1870, on some documents abandoned in Sedan that were discovered in 1896, and on some papers belonging to a man named Toussaint who headed the commissariat for the Cent-Gardes.

Viel-Castel, Comte Horace de, *Memoirs*, 2 vols., London: Remington, 1888. The assistant superintendent of the Louvre, an outstanding busybody and gossip, a master of the scurrilous. Opinion differs on his reliability. Handle with care.

Vingt Ans de Police, Souvenirs et anecdotes d'un ancien officier de paix, Paris: E. Dentu, 1881. This anonymous work must be used cautiously, but it does contain useful hints about the Paris police in the Second Empire.

Vizetelly, Ernest Alfred, *Court Life of the Second French Empire*, New York: Charles Scribner's Sons, 1907. As an extremely young newspaper reporter, Vizetelly covered the Franco-Prussian War for several papers, then fought with the French forces south of the Loire. Although his book was written as a memoir, he was an extensive reader of Second Empire materials after 1871 rather than an observer of events.

Washburne, E. B., *Recollections of a Minister to France 1869-1877*, New York: Charles Scribner's Sons, 1889. Of limited use for the Second Empire.

Welschinger, Henri, *La Guerre de 1870, causes et responsabilités*, 2 vols., Paris: Plon-Nourrit, 1919. While this book seems to take the form of an objective history, it is really an expanded memoir. Welschinger was an official of the Archives du Corps législatif from 1868 to 1870, then secretary-archivist to the National Assembly from 1871 to 1876. He attended all parliamentary sessions and had access to many papers. His ardent patriotism is visible and avowed.

Wikoff, Henry, *The Reminiscences of an Idler*, New York: Fords, Howard, & Hulbert, 1880. A Philadelphian, Wikoff first met Louis-Napoleon in Britain in 1840 and was fascinated by him.

MEDICAL ARTICLES AND BOOKS

Of the numerous medical journals consulted for this study, let us note in particular *la Chronique médicale*. Its forty-five volumes between 1893 and 1938 were edited by Dr. Augustin Cabanès, who took a special interest in the case of Napoleon III. Cabanès wrote extensively under his own name and under the pseudonym Dr. Bienvenu.

Anger, Dr. Théophile, *Siège de Paris*, Paris: A. Parent, 1871. A report on the field hospital operated by the Marquis of Hertford. Anger (often misspelled Auger), a student of Nélaton, accompanied Napoleon III at Sedan.

Cabanès, Dr. Augustin, "La mort de Napoléon III est-elle due au chloroforme?" *la Chronique médicale*, III (June 15, 1896), 353-357.

Les Morts mystérieuses de l'histoire, 2 vols., Paris: A. Michel, 1923-1927. The section on Napoleon III in II, 405-429.

Callamand, Dr. E., "A propos de la mort de Napoléon III," *la Chronique médicale*, VIII (March 1, July 15, Sept. 1, 1901), 153-154, 463-464, 558-559.

Copeman, Dr. W.S.C., *A Short History of the Gout and the Rheumatic Diseases*, Berkeley and Los Angeles: University of California Press, 1964. Intelligent and readable.

Corlieu, Dr. A., *La Mort des rois de France depuis François Ier*, Paris: Honoré Champion, 1892. The section on Napoleon III is largely based on articles in *Lancet* and on Guillon, Sée, and Corvisart.

Corvisart, Dr. Baron, "A propos de la mort de Napoléon III," *la Chronique médicale*, III (July 1, 1896), 413-416.

Critchley, Dr. Macdonald, "A Medical History of Napoleon III," *Second Empire Medley*, ed. by W. H. Holden, London: British Technical and General Press, 1952. A short but useful article. Presumably he saw Ferguson's case-report, though he spelled his name Fergusson; he thought it contained no "disclosures of a psychiatric character so attractive nowadays to the lay writer."

Dansette, Adrien, "La Maladie de Napoléon III," *la Revue de Paris*, LXX (September 1963), 35-49. Another brief and undocumented survey that contains a good current statement of the traditional views of Napoleon's case. Dr. Guy Godlewski reviewed the evidence for Dansette.

Darimon, Alfred, "La Maladie de l'empereur," which is Chapter II in his *Notes pour servir à l'histoire de la guerre de 1870*, Paris: Paul Ollendorff, 1888. A journalist who was one of les Cinq elected in 1857, Darimon contributed to the formation of the Third Party and became reconciled to the empire. He left public life in 1869.

Debout d'Estrées, Dr. Albert-Émile, *Les Causes de la gravelle et de la pierre étudiées à Contrexéville pendant neuf années de pratique médicale*, Paris: V.-A. Delahaye, 1876. He had views on Napoleon's case that were utilized by Dr. Cabanès. Debout also wrote a *Medical Guide to Contrexéville (Vosges)*, London: Churchill, 1883.

Deguison, Dr. Jean, *Napoléon III et Vichy*, Paris: G. Doin, 1934. One of the many works that confuses Doctors Guillon and Guyon.

Fauchon, Dr., "Toujours à propos de la mort de Napoléon III," *la Chronique médicale*, VIII (March 15, 1901), 191.

Faure, Dr. Jean-Louis, *En marge de la chirurgie*, 2 vols., Paris: Les Arts et Le Livre, 1927. The first volume contains a good study of Dr. Félix Guyon.

Fritsche, G., ["Account of the decease of Napoleon III," in Polish], *Medycyna*, I (1873), 65-69.

Gannat, Dr., "Les Cures de Napoléon III à Vichy," *la Chronique médicale*, XVII (Aug. 15, 1910), 559. A chamber-of-commerce defense of Vichy waters.

Gélineau, Dr., "La mort de Napoléon III," *la Chronique médicale*, VIII (Feb. 15, 1901), 127-128.

Gilbert, Judson B., *Disease and Destiny: A Bibliography*, London: Dawsons of Pall Mall, 1962.

Guépin, Dr. A., "La maladie, l'opération et la mort de Napoleon III," *la Chronique médicale*, VIII (Jan. 15, 1901), 33-44; and "A propos de la mort de Napoléon III," *ibid.*, VIII (March 1, 1901), 154-158.

Guillon, Dr. François-Gabriel, letter to *le Courrier médical*, XIX (Oct. 16, 1869), 327-328. Written to clarify what had happened at Vichy in 1866. Also see Guillon's *Œuvres chirurgicales et médicales du docteur Guillon père*, Paris: Baillière et fils, 1879.

Hassall, Dr. Arthur Hill, Letter to *Lancet*, I (Jan. 18, 1873), 113. A response to the published autopsy of Napoleon III.

Haumonté, Jean-Dominique, *Plombières ancien et moderne*, Paris: Champion, 1905.

James, Dr. Constantin, *Des causes de la mort de l'empereur*, Paris: Masson, 1873. A specialist at Vichy who was critical of Sir Henry Thompson. Also see his *Guide pratique aux eaux minérales de la France et de l'étranger*, Paris: Bloud et Barral, 1896.

Jones, Dr. Ernest, "The Case of Louis Bonaparte," *Journal of Abnormal Psychology*, VIII (Dec. 1913-Jan. 1914), 289-301. A brief but useful study of King Louis of Holland.

Kastener, Jean, "Napoléon III à Plombières," *le Pays lorrain* (Nancy), XLVII (1966), 103-119. A popular illustrated article largely based on newspaper accounts.

Lapeyrère, Dr. J., "A propos de la maladie de Napoléon III," *la France médicale*, XX (Jan. 15, 1873), 25-28; reprinted in *la Revue médicale* (March 9, 1874), 313-318.

Latour, Dr. Amadée, "Le calcul vésical de l'ex-empereur Napoléon III," *l'Union médicale*, XV (Jan. 1873), 25-27. The first publication of Dr. Sée's case-report of 1870.

Lecomte, G.-C.-N., *Napoléon III: sa maladie, son déclin*, Lyon: les Laboratoires Ciba, 1937. Based upon Cabanès and James, and probably the source of Dansette's speculation about venereal disease.

Lemaire, Dr. J.-C., "Des Médecins sous le second empire: #2 des chirurgiens," *Bulletin interne des Amis de Napoléon III*, #8 (Dec. 1968), 3-14.

Marwood, Dr. S. F., "Louis Napoleon and his Doctors," *Medical Journal of the Southwest* (Bristol), LXXXII (Jan. 1967), 71-82. This is a published presidential address delivered to the Bristol Medico-Chirugical Society on Oct. 12, 1966. We have again Dr. Fergusson.

Pariset, Dr., "Quelques notes sur les cures de Napoléon III à Vichy," *la Chronique médicale*, XVII (April 1, 1910), 209-213. More chamber-of-commerce prejudices.

Power, D'A., "Bygone operations in surgery: V. Lithotrity: the case of the Emperor Napoleon III," *British Journal of Surgery*, XIX (July 1931), 1-7. A good brief account of the origins of lithotrity and an accurate description of Napoleon's case.

Rochon, Dr. (pseud. of Dr. Coorhn), *Des Moyens rationnels de guérison immédiate des retrécissements de l'uètre et de leurs complications*, Paris: E. Dentu, 1873. A student of Dr. Civiale. This was a pamphlet to advertise the possibilities for quick and immediate relief of constricted urinary passages, and makes reference to Napoleon III's illness.

Sécheyron, Dr., "La vérité sur la maladie de Napoléon III," *la Chronique médicale*, VIII (March 15, June 15, Aug. 15, 1901), 190, 391-392, 526-528.

Sée, Dr. E.-Germain, "Un grain de sable dans la vessie d'un empereur," *la Mercure de France*, 292 (June 15, 1939), 595-598. The article was stimulated by a municipal decision to name a street in the XVIe Arrondissement after the Dr. Sée of 1870.

Sée, Dr. Germain, "Le calcul vésical de l'ex-empereur Napoléon III," *Journal des connaissances médicales pratiques*, XL (Jan. 1873), 7-9. Another publication of the 1870 case-report.

Stevenson, R. Scott, *Famous Illnesses in History*, London: Eyre & Spottiswoode, 1962. Chapter VII is on Napoleon III. We have again "Dr. Fergusson" and "Dr. Auger," suggesting far too great a dependence upon secondary sources.

Thompson, Sir Henry, "Une lettre du Dr. Thompson sur la mort de Napoléon III," *la Chronique médicale*, III (July 15, 1896), 445-446. Also see the 8th edition of Thompson's *Clinical Lectures on Diseases of the Urinary Organs*, London: Churchill, 1888, pp. 305 ff.

Treue, Wilhelm, *Doctor at Court*, New York: Roy, 1958. Very brief and very unreliable.

Wilson, Dr. J. A., Letter to *Lancet*, I (Jan. 18, 1873), 113-114. Another response to the published autopsy of Napoleon III.

Wilson, John, *Studies of Modern Mind and Character*, London: Longmans, Green, 1881. He covers Napoleon III on pp. 327-346. Inadequately informed.

Witkowski, Dr. Gustave-J.-A., *Comment moururent les rois de France*, Paris: Bibliothèque des Curieux, 1920. A brief account of Napoleon III's case and critical of Cabanès.

The weakness of Witkowski's argument lies in his unwillingness to believe that eminent physicians can make mistakes.

BIOGRAPHICAL STUDIES

In the determination of which titles should be included in this list, my principle of selection has been special relevance to Napoleon III's health and character, and to the physicians who treated him. A few of the following titles are well known, but many are rather obscure. Titles are arranged alphabetically by subject rather than by author.

[Albert] Theodore Martin, *Life of the Prince Consort*, 5 vols., London: Smith, Elder, 1875-1880. Prince Albert held dark suspicions about Napoleon's character and policies.

[Andral] Dr. Pierre Astruc, "Andral (Gabriel) 1797-1876," *les Biographies médicales*, IX (Jan. 1935), 193-208; and Georges Daremberg, *Les Grands médecins du XIXe siècle*, Paris: Masson, 1907, pp. 151-160.

[Arese] Giuseppe Grabinski, *Un Ami de Napoléon III. Le comte Arese et la politique italienne sous le second empire*, Paris: L. Bahl, 1897. Arese was a devoted friend of Napoleon III and visited Camden Place.

[Bonapartes] Theo Aronson, *The Golden Bees, the Story of the Bonapartes*, Greenwich, Conn.: New York Graphic Society, 1964. Popular and unreliable.

[Bouillaud] Dr. Paul Busquet, "Bouillaud (Jean-Baptiste)," *les Biographies médicales*, V (Jan. 1931), 311-324; and Dr. Henri-Georges Dejeant, *La Vie et l'œuvre de Bouillaud*, Paris: Louis Arnette, 1930.

[Canrobert] Germain Bapst, *Le Maréchal Canrobert. Souvenirs d'un siècle*, 4 vols., Paris: Plon, 1903-1904.

[Castiglione] Alain Decaux, *La Castiglione, Dame de cœur de l'Europe*, Paris: Amiot-Dupont, 1953.

[Cloquet] Dr. Maurice Genty, "Cloquet (Jules-Germain) 1790-1883," *les Biographies médicales*, VII (Jan. 1933), 261-273.

[Conneau] Marcel de Baillehache, *Grands Bonapartistes*, Paris: Tallandier, 1899; and Marc de Fontbrune, "Le docteur Conneau, médecin de Napoléon III," *Miroir de l'histoire*, #130 (1960), 470-476, a popular article with good illustrations.

[Cornu] Marcel Emerit, *Madame Cornu et Napoléon III*, Paris: Les Presses Modernes, 1937. He has used the correspondence of Napoleon to Mme. Cornu now in the Bibliothèque Nationale. Highly antagonistic to the emperor.

[Darboy] Joseph-Alfred, Cardinal Foulon, *Histoire de la vie et des œuvres de Monseigneur Darboy*, Paris: Poussielgue, 1889. Darboy was present at Saint-Cloud to say Mass before Napoleon left for the front in 1870 and noted the pessimistic atmosphere.

[Eugénie] Maurice, Comte Fleury, *Memoirs of the Empress Eugénie*, 2 vols., New York: D. Appleton, 1920. A very pro-Bonapartist work which contains important information. Edward Legge, *The Empress Eugénie 1870-1910*, London and New York: Harper & Bros., 1910. Legge attributed his medical information to Dr. Debout d'Estrées, and he used (and disputed) the Comte de La Chapelle. The latest and most favorable biography is Harold Kurtz, *The Empress Eugénie 1826-1920*, London: Hamish Hamilton, 1964.

[Evans] M. L. Charenton, *Le Docteur Thomas W. Evans, dentiste de Napoléon III et les dentistes de son époque*, Paris: Le François, 1936. Much of the information about Evans can be found in fuller form in his own memoirs.

[Granville] Lord Edmond Fitzmaurice, *Life of Earl Granville* (Granville George Leveson Gower, second Earl), 2 vols., London: Longmans, Green, 1905. Foreign minister after the *coup d'état* of 1851 for several months, and again in June, 1870, after Clarendon's death.

[Guyon] Dr. A. Gosset, *Chirurgie, chirurgiens*, Paris: Gallimard, 1941. Contains a section on Dr. Félix Guyon, one of Gosset's professors.

[Howard] Simone André Maurois, *Miss Howard and the Emperor*, New York: Alfred Knopf, 1957. She corrects much misinformation about the emperor's mistress.

[Jobert] Dr. Maurice Genty, "Jobert (de Lamballe), Antoine-Joseph 1802-1867," *les Biographies médicales*, v (Oct. 1931), 17-32.

[Larrey] Dr. L.-J.-B. Bérenger-Féraud, *Le Baron Hippolyte Larrey (1808-1895)*, Paris: Fayard frères, 1899. The author had the use of the Larrey papers when they were still in the possession of Mlle. Juliette Dodu. See also J. de Fourmestraux, "Hippolyte Larrey," *les Biographies médicales*, x (Oct. 1936), 241-256, which includes a useful bibliography.

[Lebœuf] Erwan Marec, "Un fils de Napoléon III à Lorient (Charles Lebœuf)," *les Cahiers de l'Iroise* (Brest), new series, xiv, #41 (1967), 255. A poorly-informed article.

[Lyons] Thomas Wodehouse Legh, Lord Newton, *Life of Lord Lyons*, 2 vols., London: Longmans, Green, 1913. The British ambassador who followed Cowley in Paris in 1867.

[MacMahon] Léon Laforge, *Histoire complète de MacMahon*, 3 vols., Paris: Lamulle et Poisson, 1898. Partisan, but based on much documentary material.

[Mathilde] Marguerite Castillon du Perron, *La Princesse Mathilde, un règne féminin sous le Second Empire*, Paris: Amiot-Dumont, 1953. Supersedes all other biographies. She had the use of Mathilde's correspondence willed to Count Joseph Primoli, and by him to the Countess Guglielmina Campello of Rome.

[Napoleon III] Edmond Bapst, *Projets de mariage de Napoléon III*, Paris: A. Lahure, 1921. This Bapst, a relative of Germain Bapst, was a professional diplomatist.

W. Beatty-Kingston, *Monarchs I Have Met*, 2 vols., London: Chapman & Hall, 1887. The first volume has material on Napoleon III.

Dr. R. Benard, "Bâtards de Napoléon III," *Chercheurs et curieux*, iv, #39 (1954), 288. The author knew Dr. Hugenschmidt.

Jules Bertaut, *Napoléon III secret,* Paris: B. Grasset, 1939. No bibliography, but a few footnotes refer to well-known secondary sources. The illness is discussed in conventional terms: The emperor's health was ruined by "excesses of all sorts." Yet Bertaut is favorable to the emperor.

General Henri Bonnal, *Le Haut commandement français au début de chacune des guerres de 1859 et de 1870: étude sur la psychologie militaire de Napoléon III en 1859 . . . et de Bazaine en 1870*, Paris: R. Chapelot, 1905. The work is heavily indebted to Bapst's work on Canrobert. Bonnal's rough thesis is that the defects in the French command in 1859 were obscured by success, but were the same defects that were fatal in 1870.

Dr. Augustin Cabanès, *Moeurs intimes du passé: Education de princes*, Paris: A. Michel, 1923. Revealing on the childhood of Louis-Napoleon.

Duc M.-J.-P. de Cambacérès, *Funérailles de Napoléon III*, Paris: Librairie Générale, 1873. The *procès-verbal* by the grand maître des cérémonies.

T.A.B. Corley, *Democratic Despot, a Life of Napoleon III*, London: Barrie & Rockliff, 1961. The best of modern biographies of Napoleon III, containing an excellent bibliography; and not well enough known in this country, perhaps because it was never reviewed here.

Adrien Dansette, *Les Amours de Napoléon III*, Paris: Fayard, 1938. A popular work telling the well-known stories but missing the intimate details of the marriage.

Suzanne Desternes and Henriette Chandet, *Napoléon III, homme du XX*^e^ *siècle*, Paris: Hachette, 1961. A study of the emperor as a modernizer, a social reformer, and the precursor of the twentieth-century international organizers.

Hector Fleishmann, *Napoleon III and the Women He Loved*, London: Holden & Hardingham, 1915. Must be used with caution. Some of his errors about Miss Howard have been corrected by Ivor Guest and by Mme. Maurois.

Fernand Giraudeau, *La Mort et les funérailles de Napoléon III*, Paris: Amyot, 1873; and *Napoléon III intime*, Paris: Paul Ollendorff, 1895. Giraudeau was a Bonapartist publicist, sometimes using the pseudonym André Raibaud. Under the Second Empire he was an officer in the ministry of the interior, and he had access to important sources.

Paul Guériot, *La Captivité de Napoléon III en Allemagne (Septembre 1870–Mars 1871)*, Paris: Perrin, 1926. See also his *Napoléon III*, 2 vols., Paris: Payot, 1933-1934.

Ivor Guest, *Napoleon III in England*, London: British Technical and General Press, 1952.

Blanchard Jerrold, *The Life of Napoleon III*, 4 vols., London: Longmans, Green, 1874-1882. The authorized life. The first two volumes are much more reliable than the final two, but Emerit thinks poorly of Jerrold's translations of Napoleon's letters.

Melvin Kranzberg, "An Emperor Writes History," in H. Stuart Hughes, *Teachers of History: Essays in Honor of L. B. Packard*, Ithaca: Cornell University Press, 1954. Amusing and well done.

André Lebey, *Les Trois coups d'état de Louis-Napoléon Bonaparte*, Paris: Perrin, 1906. He has a good section on the period at Ham.

Mitarra, "La descendance naturelle de Napoléon III," *la Vie judiciaire*, #365 (1953), 9. Mostly gossip.

Henri Welschinger, "La Captivité de Napoléon III à Wilhelmshöhe (5 septembre 1870–mars 1871)," *Revue des deux mondes*, LVI (March-April 1910), 621-644, 901-925. He relies heavily on Monts and Mels.

[Rayer] Dr. Raoul Caveribert, *La Vie et l'œuvre de Rayer (1793-1867)*, Paris: Marcel Vigné, 1931; and Dr. Maurice

Genty, "Rayer (Pierre-François-Olive) 1793-1867," *les Biographies médicales*, v (Nov. 1931), 33-48.

[Ricord] Dr. A. Riant, *Le Dr. Philippe Ricord*, Paris: Alcan-Lévy, 1889. Actually a brief eulogy pronounced at Père Lachaise.

[Tardieu] Dr. René Semelaigne, *Les Pionniers de la psychiatrie française avant et après Pinel*, 2 vols., Paris: Baillière et fils, 1932. Vol. II contains a brief section on Dr. Auguste Tardieu.

[Thompson] Sir Zachary Cope, *The Versatile Victorian: Being the Life of Sir Henry Thompson*, London: Harvey and Blythe, 1951. Sir Zachary had the use of Thompson's journal.

[Velpeau] Dr. Maurice Genty, "Velpeau (Marie) 1795-1867," *les Biographies médicales*, v (April-May 1931), 357-384.

[Vergeot] Roger Régis, *La Belle Sabotière et le prisonnier de Ham*, Paris: Editions de France, 1937. A novel that is faintly historical.

[Walewski] Philippe Poirson, *Walewski, fils de Napoléon*, Paris: Editions Balzac, 1943; Françoise Chalamon de Bernardy, *Un Fils de Napoléon: le comte Walewski, 1810-1868*, an unpublished doctoral thesis at Paris, 1951; and Comte d'Orano, *La Vie passionante du comte Walewski, fils de Napoléon*, Paris: Les Editions Comtales, 1953. Orano was a nephew of Mme. Walewska, née Ricci, and had the use of family papers.

POLITICAL TRACTS

Allart, Marcus, *Un Electeur à son retour de Chislehurst*, Versailles and Brussels: Librairie Générale, 1873. A political pamphlet demanding a Bonaparte restoration. An example of anti-Republican crank literature.

Amigues, Jules, *La Mort de Napoléon III*, Paris: F. Debons, 1877. A reprint from the *Droit du Peuple*, of which Amigues was chief editor. Bonapartist propaganda recalling the anniversary of the emperor's death.

Bibliography

Anselme, A., *Les Idées de l'empereur Napoléon III*, Paris: J. Garnier, 1863. A nine-page piece of wretched verse celebrating the emperor and his programs, by a primary-school inspector—a real "Homais."

Attentats et complots contre Napoléon III, histoire complète des attentats et des complots, Paris: Chevalier, 1870. An anonymous tract written shortly before the fall of the empire. It contains useful names and descriptions.

Bellanger, Marguerite, *Les Amours de Napoléon III, mémoires de Marguerite Bellanger*, Paris: P. Fort, 1900. An apocryphal work unflattering to the emperor.

Blanc, Louis, *L'Empire moins l'empereur, lettre à Louis Bonaparte*, n.p., n.d. The letter was originally written on Aug. 10, 1849, recalling Blanc's visit to Ham and to remind the new president how once before he had fallen into the trap of his imperial illusions. This is a reprint, published shortly after the coup d'état of 1851 as a warning against overthrowing the Second Republic.

Blétry, Pauline, *Napoléon III et sa bonté*, Paris: Henri Jouve, 1910. A peculiar pamphlet, originally a speech, to remind the working classes of the benevolent despotism of Napoleon III. An anti-Republican tract.

Claude, Antoine-François, *Mémoires de Monsieur Claude, chef de la police de Sureté sous le second empire*, 10 vols., Paris: Jules Rouff, 1881-1882. A spurious work, author unknown. But he was a skillful polemicist, treating Napoleon III as the eternal and masterful conspirator. The work was clearly intended to boost the reputation of Adolphe Thiers. Another object was to show that the various aristocratic lovers of His Majesty were all foreign agents and traitors, thus linking the imperial escapades to the defeat of 1870. While the work was identified even in the nineteenth century as a fraud, it has been reprinted in abridged form by the so-called Amis de l'histoire, Paris, 1968, with an introductory assurance that "Rien ne permet de douter de leur authenticité." Claude's real papers went to Macé, his successor.

Flammarion, Dr. Jules, *Une Page d'histoire contemporaine: le bonapartisme*, Gap: Les Editions Napoléoniennes, 1950. Pro-Bonapartist and very amateur, but an interesting example of lingering Bonapartism.

Griscelli de Vezzani, Jacques-François, *Mémoires*, Geneva, Brussels, and London: 1867. (No publisher admits it!) Griscelli, a notoriously corrupt Corsican, often signed himself the Baron de Rimini. This is a very unreliable source. His *Les Crimes politiques de Napoléon III*, Paris: Librairie Centrale, 1873, was a brief extension of his *Mémoires* in which he repeats some of the earlier material, but adds more vicious lies in the hope of finding employment in the police of the Third Republic.

Hérisson, Maurice d'Irisson, Comte d', *Les Responsabilités de l'année terrible*, Paris: Paul Ollendorff, 1891. A naked attempt to rehabilitate Bazaine.

Loudun, Eugène, *Étude sur les œuvres de Napoléon III*, Paris: Amyot, 1857. Originally published in *le Constitutionnel*, Nov. 28-29, 1856. Most princes have written little, he asserts. But those who have written most have been the most illustrious (Caesar, Frederick II, Louis XIV, and Napoleon I) and whom we call "the Great." We are to understand that Napoleon III's voluminous writing amounts to a prediction of grandeur. Publish or perish.

Magen, Hippolyte, *Les deux Courts et les nuits de Saint-Cloud*, London: Jeffs, 1852; and *Les Femmes galantes des Napoléon, secrets de cour et de palais*, London and Geneva, 1865. Nothing but dirt hurled from abroad.

Napoleon III, *Souvenirs et notes intimes de Napoléon III à Wilhelmshöhe*, Paris: Librairie Internationale, 1871. A spurious work, possibly written by Henri de Kock and Adolphe Jaime.

Sosthène-Berthellot, C., *Essai sur le caractère et les tendences de l'Empereur Napoléon III d'après ses écrits et ses actes*, Paris: Henri Plon, 1858. A eulogistic, documentary biography, with a good table of contents to make the documents easily available to the reader.

Index

Index

Index

Index